Building modern web applications using PHP

Revised, September 2025

Dr Alex Bugeja, PhD

Table of Contents

Introduction

There's a persistent rumor in the web development world, a ghost story told around the virtual campfire of social media and tech blogs. It goes something like this: "PHP is dead." This declaration often comes with a knowing nod, as if sharing some profound, insider secret. The irony is that this eulogy has been delivered, year after year, for the better part of a decade. Yet, like a resilient protagonist in a never-ending action movie, PHP refuses to stay down. The simple, unvarnished truth is that PHP is not dead. It's not even unwell. In fact, it's more mature, faster, and more capable than it has ever been.

Reports of PHP's demise are greatly exaggerated, and the data backs this up. As of early 2025, PHP is the engine behind a staggering percentage of the web. Statistics show that it is used by 73.4% to 77.4% of all websites whose server-side programming language is known. This isn't a small, niche player; it's the foundational technology for a vast portion of the internet. Much of this dominance is thanks to Content Management Systems (CMS) like WordPress, which itself powers over 43% of all websites. While some developers might dismiss this as the inertia of the past, it's impossible to ignore the reality of its footprint. Millions of businesses, from small blogs to large enterprises, rely on PHP every single day.

The language's journey began in 1994, when Rasmus Lerdorf created a set of scripts to manage his personal homepage. These "Personal Home Page Tools," or PHP Tools, were never intended to become a global phenomenon. Yet, their utility was undeniable. Over the years, with the help of developers like Zeev Suraski and Andi Gutmans, PHP evolved from a simple set of tools into a full-fledged scripting language. Versions like PHP 3 and 4 introduced more robust features and object-oriented programming capabilities, while PHP 5, launched in 2004, solidified its position with the powerful Zend Engine II and greatly improved OOP support.

However, the real revolution, the one that silenced many critics and laid the foundation for the modern era, arrived with PHP 7 in 2015. This version brought with it a massive leap in performance, in some cases doubling the speed of applications and drastically reducing memory consumption. It was a clear signal that PHP was not content to rest on its laurels. The innovations continued with PHP 8, which introduced the Just-In-Time (JIT) compiler, a feature that can significantly boost performance for certain types of computationally intensive tasks by compiling parts of the code into machine code at runtime. This evolution is a testament to the vibrant community and the PHP Foundation, which work to ensure the language not only keeps pace with but also helps to define modern web development.

So, what exactly do we mean by "modern PHP"? It's a term that signifies a fundamental shift away from the practices of the early 2000s. The PHP of today is a different beast entirely. It's a language that embraces strong typing, elegant object-oriented principles, and a clean, consistent syntax. Modern PHP development is characterized by a rich ecosystem of tools and practices that promote robust, maintainable, and scalable applications. It is a world away from the single-file, spaghetti-code scripts that gave the language its early, and somewhat unfair, reputation.

At the heart of this modern ecosystem is Composer, the dependency manager for PHP. Before Composer, managing external libraries was a messy, manual process. Developers had to download files, place them in the correct directories, and handle autoloading themselves. Composer changed everything. It provides a standardized way to declare, install, and manage project dependencies, pulling in high-quality, reusable components from Packagist, the central package repository. This has fostered a culture of sharing and collaboration, allowing developers to build complex applications by standing on the shoulders of giants.

Another cornerstone of modern PHP is the work of the PHP Framework Interop Group (PHP-FIG). This group has been instrumental in establishing a set of common standards, known as

PSRs (PHP Standard Recommendations). These standards cover everything from coding style (PSR-12) and autoloading (PSR-4) to common interfaces for things like HTTP messages (PSR-7) and caching (PSR-6). By creating these shared conventions, PSRs allow for a high degree of interoperability between different frameworks and components, making it easier for developers to mix and match tools to suit their needs.

This book is written for a specific kind of developer. Perhaps you're new to web development and have heard the whispers about PHP, but you're curious about a language that powers so much of the web. Maybe you're a developer coming from another language, like Python or JavaScript, and you want to understand what the modern PHP ecosystem has to offer. Or, perhaps you are a seasoned PHP developer who learned the craft in an earlier era and wants to update your skills to reflect current best practices, moving from legacy code to modern, robust applications. This book is for you.

We will assume you have a basic understanding of programming concepts. You should know what a variable is, what a loop does, and the general idea behind a function. We're not going to spend time explaining the fundamentals of programming itself. Instead, our focus will be squarely on how to apply those concepts to build professional, high-quality web applications using the latest versions and tools that PHP has to offer. This is a practical journey from the ground up, aimed at making you a confident and capable modern PHP developer.

It's also important to clarify what this book is not. It is not an exhaustive language reference manual. While we will cover the essential syntax and features of modern PHP, our goal is not to document every single function and configuration option. The official PHP documentation is excellent and serves that purpose perfectly. This book is also not a deep dive into a single, monolithic framework. While we will explore popular frameworks and use a microframework to build a RESTful API, the primary focus is on the underlying principles and components that these frameworks are built upon.

By understanding the "why" behind the patterns and tools, you'll be better equipped to choose the right framework for a given project, or even build your own solutions when necessary. We aim to teach you how to fish, not just give you a fish. The skills you learn here will be transferable across the entire PHP ecosystem, empowering you to think critically about architecture and design. We will focus on building applications that are not just functional, but also secure, performant, and a pleasure to maintain.

Our journey through this book is structured to build your knowledge progressively. We'll begin with the "Modern PHP Landscape," putting the language in its current context. From there, we'll guide you through setting up a professional development environment, a crucial first step that is often overlooked. We will then dive into the fundamentals of the language as it exists today, with PHP 8 and beyond, ensuring you start with a solid, modern foundation. You will learn about Composer for dependency management and explore advanced object-oriented programming concepts and design patterns.

As we progress, we'll move from theory to practice. You'll understand the MVC (Model-View-Controller) pattern and how modern frameworks are structured. We'll get our hands dirty by building a RESTful API, learning about routing, middleware, and controllers. We'll explore how to interact with databases effectively using both raw PDO and Object-Relational Mappers (ORMs). Subsequent chapters will cover essential topics like user authentication, templating engines, form validation, and security best practices to protect your application from common threats.

The final third of the book pushes into more advanced and specialized territory. We'll look at how to build high-performance applications through caching strategies and explore asynchronous PHP for real-time features with WebSockets. We will cover the critical discipline of testing, from unit tests to end-to-end testing. Finally, we'll take a broader look at the application lifecycle, covering containerization with Docker, interacting with third-party services, and setting up a Continuous Integration and Continuous Deployment (CI/CD) pipeline for automated, reliable deployments. We even peek into the future with serverless PHP and strategies for scaling your application.

So, why should you choose PHP for your next project in 2025? The reasons are as compelling as they are practical. The language has evolved into a high-performance tool, with benchmarks for PHP 8 often competing favorably with other popular backend languages like Node.js and Python in many common web scenarios. The massive community means that you are never far from an answer. An extensive ecosystem of libraries, frameworks, and tools means you rarely have to reinvent the wheel.

Furthermore, the barrier to entry for deployment remains remarkably low. PHP hosting is ubiquitous and affordable, making it an excellent choice for projects of all sizes, from a personal blog to a scalable SaaS platform. The simplicity of its deployment model, especially in traditional environments, allows developers to get applications up and running with minimal friction. This combination of performance, a mature ecosystem, a large talent pool, and ease of deployment makes PHP a pragmatic and powerful choice for building for the web.

This book adopts a philosophy of pragmatism and professionalism. Our goal is to teach you the best practices that lead to clean, maintainable, and robust code. We believe that building software is a craft, and like any craft, it requires a commitment to quality and a deep understanding of one's tools. We will cut through the noise and focus on the principles that matter, providing you with the knowledge to build applications you can be proud of. There's a world of difference between code that simply works and code that is well-designed, and our focus is squarely on the latter.

The web development landscape is constantly in flux, with new technologies and trends emerging at a dizzying pace. It can be tempting to chase the latest shiny object. However, beneath the surface of these trends are foundational principles of good software design that remain timeless. By mastering the modern PHP ecosystem, you are not just learning a programming language; you are learning a set of skills and practices that will serve you well throughout your career, regardless of the specific technologies you use.

This book is your guide to that ecosystem. It's a roadmap to understanding not just how to write PHP code, but how to think like a modern PHP developer. We will tackle complex topics, but we will do so one step at a time, building a comprehensive picture from the ground up. Whether you are taking your first steps into backend development or are looking to modernize a valuable skill set, you have chosen a powerful and relevant path. The journey ahead is an exciting one, filled with challenges and rewards. Let's begin.

CHAPTER ONE: The Modern PHP Landscape

To understand where PHP is in 2025, you first have to appreciate where it's been. The language has undergone a remarkable transformation, evolving from a simple tool for creating dynamic web pages into a sophisticated, high-performance engine for complex applications. This journey wasn't always smooth. For years, PHP carried the baggage of its early days—a reputation for messy, unstructured code and inconsistent function names. But to judge the PHP of today by the standards of 2005 would be like judging a modern electric car by the standards of a Ford Model T. They both have wheels, but the underlying technology, philosophy, and performance are worlds apart. The modern PHP landscape is defined by structure, professionalism, and an incredibly rich ecosystem that promotes building software that is not only functional but also robust, scalable, and maintainable.

This transformation began at the very core of the language. The single most significant event in PHP's modern history was the release of PHP 7 in 2015. It wasn't just another version; it was a quantum leap. Under the hood, the Zend Engine was almost completely rewritten, resulting in staggering performance gains. Applications saw their speed double or even triple overnight, with a simultaneous reduction in memory usage. This wasn't a minor tune-up; it was a complete engine overhaul. The improvements have continued steadily with each subsequent release. PHP 8 brought further optimizations and introduced the Just-In-Time (JIT) compiler. While the JIT compiler offers the most significant benefits for long-running scripts and computationally intensive tasks rather than typical web requests, its inclusion was a powerful statement of intent about the language's future direction.

Equally important is the professionalization of the language's development and release cycle. Gone are the days of unpredictable releases. PHP now follows a predictable, annual release schedule, with a new version arriving toward the end of each year. This clockwork-like regularity gives developers, businesses, and hosting providers a clear roadmap for the future, allowing them to plan upgrades and manage deprecations effectively. Furthermore, the establishment of The PHP Foundation in late 2021 has been a watershed moment. Supported by major companies in the PHP ecosystem like JetBrains, Automattic, Laravel, and Symfony, the foundation's mission is to ensure the long-term prosperity of the language. It does this by funding core developers to work on maintenance, bug fixes, and new features, ensuring the language is not just surviving but actively thriving under a stable and well-funded stewardship.

Perhaps the single greatest catalyst in PHP's evolution into a modern language was the introduction of Composer in 2012. Before Composer, managing dependencies—the external libraries and components your project relies on—was a chaotic, manual process. Developers would download zip files, extract them into a `vendor` or `includes` directory, and then write a series of `require_once` statements to load them. This was brittle, hard to update, and made sharing code between projects a nightmare. It was a world of isolated castles, each with its own set of rules and manually curated libraries. Composer, and its companion repository Packagist, tore down those castle walls and built a global superhighway for PHP code.

Composer is a dependency manager. It allows you to declare the libraries your project needs in a simple JSON file, `composer.json`. With a single command, `composer install`, it will find the correct versions of those packages from Packagist, resolve their dependencies, download them into a standardized `vendor` directory, and—this is the crucial part—set up a universal autoloader. This means you no longer have to manually include files. As long as a library follows modern standards, Composer handles everything. This seemingly simple utility had a profound impact. It fostered a culture of creating small, reusable, single-purpose packages. Developers could now easily pull in a high-quality library for logging, routing, sending emails, or interacting with a third-party API, confident that it would integrate smoothly into their project.

Packagist is the public repository that Composer connects to by default. It is the largest repository of PHP packages in the world, hosting hundreds of thousands of open-source libraries. This vast ecosystem means that for almost any common problem you might face in web development, there's likely already a well-tested, community-vetted package available. This allows developers to focus on building the unique features of their application instead of reinventing the wheel. The combination of Composer and Packagist fundamentally shifted the paradigm of PHP development from writing everything from scratch to assembling applications from high-quality, interoperable components. It is the bedrock upon which the entire modern ecosystem is built.

If Composer provided the "how" of sharing code, the PHP Framework Interoperability Group (PHP-FIG) provided the "what." Formed by representatives from major PHP frameworks and projects, the group's goal was to solve a persistent problem: while projects could now share code via Composer, they often couldn't work together because they had different ways of doing the same thing. One framework might have its own way of handling HTTP requests, while another had a completely different approach. This fragmentation made it difficult to mix and match components from different projects. The PHP-FIG set out to create a series of common standards, or PHP Standard Recommendations (PSRs), to promote interoperability.

These PSRs are not part of the PHP language itself; they are community-driven specifications that define common interfaces for essential concepts. For example, PSR-4 defines a standard way for autoloaders to map namespaces to file paths, which is the convention that allows Composer's autoloader to work so seamlessly. PSR-12 is an extended coding style guide, replacing the older PSR-2, which helps ensure that code looks and feels consistent across different projects, reducing cognitive friction for developers.

More advanced PSRs define common interfaces for more complex components. PSR-7, for instance, standardizes how HTTP messages (requests and responses) are represented in PHP objects.

This was a game-changer, as it allowed developers to write middleware—code that intercepts and acts on a request or response—that could work with any PSR-7 compatible framework. Other important PSRs cover logging (PSR-3), caching (PSR-6 and PSR-16), and HTTP clients (PSR-18). By adhering to these standards, library authors can create components that are decoupled from any single framework, and framework authors can allow their users to bring in any PSR-compliant component they choose. This has created a virtuous cycle of collaboration and flexibility that defines the modern PHP landscape.

The modern landscape is dominated by a few key frameworks that provide the structure and tooling necessary for building large, maintainable applications. While there are many to choose from, two stand out as the giants of the ecosystem: Symfony and Laravel. Though they share many modern principles and often use the same underlying components, they represent two distinct philosophies of framework design.

Symfony is best understood as a collection of high-quality, decoupled components that can be used independently or assembled into a full-stack framework. This "Lego" approach provides immense flexibility and control, making it a favorite for large, complex, and long-term enterprise applications where architectural precision is paramount. Symfony's components are so well-regarded that they are used by many other PHP projects, including Laravel itself. It emphasizes adherence to design patterns and configurability, which can result in a steeper learning curve but offers unparalleled power for bespoke solutions. Its ecosystem includes a robust templating engine called Twig and a powerful Object-Relational Mapper (ORM) called Doctrine for database interactions.

Laravel, created by Taylor Otwell, takes a different approach. It is often described as a "batteries-included" framework that prioritizes developer experience (DX) and rapid application development. Known for its elegant and expressive syntax, Laravel provides out-of-the-box solutions for common tasks like authentication, routing, sessions, and caching. This convention-over-configuration philosophy allows developers to build functional applications incredibly quickly, making it extremely popular with startups and for projects with tight deadlines. Laravel has a massive and active community and an extensive ecosystem of first-party tools like Forge for server management and Vapor for serverless deployment, which streamline the entire development and deployment workflow.

Beyond these two giants, the landscape is rich with other options. Microframeworks like Slim and Laminas Mezzio (the successor to Zend Expressive) are designed for building smaller applications and, most notably, APIs. They provide the bare essentials, like routing and dependency injection, allowing developers to add only the components they need. At the other end of the spectrum are the massive Content Management Systems (CMS) like WordPress, Drupal, and Magento. While these platforms have a long history, they too have been profoundly influenced by the modern PHP ecosystem. They have embraced Composer for managing their dependencies, adopted modern object-oriented principles, and increasingly provide REST APIs to interact with headless frontends, proving that even the largest legacy codebases are moving in a modern direction.

The shift in mindset in the PHP community is also reflected in the professional-grade tooling that is now considered standard practice. Modern PHP development is no longer about editing a file on a live server via FTP. It involves a sophisticated local environment and a suite of tools designed to ensure code quality, correctness, and consistency. A key part of this evolution has been the rise of static analysis tools. Tools like PHPStan and Psalm inspect your code without actually running it, much like a spellchecker for grammar and syntax. They can detect a huge range of potential bugs, from simple type mismatches to complex logical errors, before the code ever reaches a testing environment. By integrating these tools into their workflow, developers can catch errors early, improve code clarity, and refactor with much greater confidence.

Alongside static analysis, a strong emphasis is placed on automated testing. PHPUnit has long been the gold standard for unit testing, providing a robust framework for verifying that individual pieces of code work as expected. More recently, frameworks like Pest have emerged, offering a more expressive and developer-friendly syntax built on top of PHPUnit. This focus on testing is a hallmark of professional software development, ensuring that applications are reliable and that new features don't break existing functionality.

Finally, maintaining a consistent code style across a project with multiple developers is crucial for readability and maintainability. Tools like PHP-CS-Fixer and Pint automate this process. They can be configured to follow a specific coding standard, such as PSR-12, and will automatically reformat code to ensure compliance. When combined, these tools—static analyzers, testing frameworks, and code style fixers—form a powerful safety net. They are typically integrated into a Continuous Integration (CI) pipeline, which automatically runs these checks every time a developer commits new code, ensuring that the quality of the main codebase remains high.

So, where does PHP fit into the broader web stack of 2025? Its role has become both more specialized and more powerful. For many applications, PHP still excels as the engine for traditional, server-rendered websites. Using powerful templating engines like Twig (popularized by Symfony) or Blade (native to Laravel), developers can build robust, full-stack applications where PHP handles everything from database queries to rendering the final HTML. This approach is simple, proven, and incredibly effective for a vast range of projects, from content-heavy sites to complex e-commerce platforms.

However, PHP has also firmly established itself as a first-class citizen in the world of APIs and microservices. In an era dominated by frontend JavaScript frameworks like React, Vue, and Angular, the backend's primary role is often to provide a fast, reliable, and secure API for the frontend to consume. Modern PHP is exceptionally well-suited for this task. Frameworks like Laravel and Symfony make it trivial to build RESTful or GraphQL APIs, handling complex routing, data transformation, and authentication with ease. The language's performance improvements mean it can handle high-throughput API requests efficiently, making it a pragmatic choice for powering Single Page Applications (SPAs) and mobile apps.

A more recent and exciting development is the rise of asynchronous PHP. Traditionally, PHP has operated on a synchronous, request-per-process model, which is simple and effective for most web tasks but less suited for long-running processes or real-time applications like chat servers or live data streams. Projects like Swoole, Amp, and ReactPHP have introduced event loops and coroutines to PHP, allowing it to handle thousands of concurrent connections and I/O-bound tasks without blocking. This opens up new possibilities for building high-performance, real-time services in PHP, a domain previously dominated by languages like Node.js. While still an emerging area, the growing adoption of asynchronous capabilities shows that the PHP ecosystem continues to innovate and expand its horizons. The modern PHP landscape is therefore not a single, monolithic entity, but a diverse and vibrant collection of powerful tools, frameworks, and philosophies, ready to tackle nearly any challenge the modern web can present.

CHAPTER TWO: Setting Up a Professional Development Environment

Before we can write a single line of modern PHP, we need to build our workshop. A craftsman is only as good as their tools, and for a software developer, the "workshop" is the development environment. This is the collection of software on your local machine—your code editor, your PHP interpreter, your local web server, and various command-line utilities—that allows you to build, test, and debug your application in a safe, controlled setting. Gone are the days of "cowboy coding," where developers would edit files directly on a live server using an FTP client. This practice was not just inefficient; it was dangerously unprofessional, akin to a mechanic trying to fix a car's engine while it's speeding down the highway.

A professional development environment serves several critical purposes. First and foremost, it provides a safety net. It allows you to experiment, break things, and fix them without any risk to the live application that your users are interacting with. Second, it ensures consistency. By creating an environment that closely mirrors the production server where your application will ultimately live, you can eliminate the dreaded "but it works on my machine" problem. Finally, a well-configured environment dramatically boosts productivity. Tools that provide intelligent code completion, powerful debugging capabilities, and automated quality checks are not luxuries; they are fundamental to writing high-quality code efficiently. In this chapter, we will walk through the process of assembling this professional toolkit, piece by piece.

Your Code Editor: The Command Center

At the heart of any developer's workflow is the code editor. This is where you will spend the vast majority of your time. While you could technically write PHP in a simple text editor like Notepad, doing so would be an exercise in frustration. Modern code editors and Integrated Development Environments (IDEs) are packed with features designed to make your life easier. They understand the syntax of your language, offer intelligent suggestions, and integrate with other tools to create a seamless development experience. In the PHP world, two choices stand out from the crowd: Visual Studio Code and PhpStorm.

Visual Studio Code, or VS Code, is a free, open-source code editor from Microsoft that has taken the development world by storm. It's lightweight, fast, and incredibly extensible. Out of the box, it's a capable editor, but its true power lies in its vast marketplace of extensions. With a few clicks, you can transform VS Code into a powerful PHP development environment. Some essential extensions to install include *PHP Intelephense* for intelligent code completion and analysis, *PHP Debug* for integrating with Xdebug, and a code formatter like *PHP CS Fixer* or *Pint* to keep your code style consistent. Its built-in terminal and Git integration mean you can perform most of your daily tasks without ever leaving the editor.

PhpStorm, developed by JetBrains, is a full-fledged IDE built specifically for PHP. Unlike VS Code, which is a general-purpose editor you configure for PHP, PhpStorm is designed from the ground up for the language and its ecosystem. It is a commercial product, but for many professional developers, the investment is well worth it. Its code analysis is second to none, providing deep insights into your codebase and enabling powerful refactoring tools that can rename a class across an entire project or automatically extract a method with a single command. It comes with a powerful debugger, a database client, a REST client, and deep integration for frameworks like Symfony and Laravel built right in. While VS Code is an excellent and highly capable choice, PhpStorm offers a more integrated, "batteries-included" experience tailored for the serious PHP professional. The choice between them often comes down to personal preference and budget, but you can't go wrong with either.

Installing and Managing PHP

Naturally, to develop with PHP, you need PHP installed on your machine. However, the modern development landscape often requires you to work on multiple projects simultaneously, and these projects may not all use the same version of PHP. One project might be running on the latest PHP 8.3, while a legacy project you're maintaining might still be on PHP 8.1. Simply installing a single version of PHP using your operating system's default package manager can quickly become a limitation. Therefore, it's crucial to use tools that allow you to install and switch between different PHP versions easily.

For macOS users, the de facto package manager is Homebrew. You can use it to install specific versions of PHP and link or unlink them as needed. For example, installing PHP 8.3 is as simple as running `brew install php@8.3`. You can then use `brew link php@8.3` to make it the active version on your command line. This gives you a good degree of control over your local PHP environment.

Windows developers have historically faced more challenges, but the situation has improved dramatically with the introduction of the Windows Subsystem for Linux (WSL). WSL allows you to run a genuine Linux environment directly on Windows, providing access to the same powerful command-line tools that Linux and macOS users enjoy. Setting up a development environment within WSL is often the recommended approach for serious PHP development on Windows. For those looking for a native Windows solution, tools like Laragon provide a complete, isolated development environment that is easy to install and manage. It bundles a web server, multiple PHP versions, a database, and other essential tools into a single, cohesive package.

On Linux, you can certainly use your distribution's package manager (like `apt` on Debian/Ubuntu or `yum` on CentOS). For more flexibility in managing multiple versions, you can use repositories like the PPA maintained by Ondřej Surý for Ubuntu, which provides multiple, up-to-date PHP versions that can be installed side-by-side. Tools like `phpbrew` offer an even finer level of control, allowing you to compile and manage different PHP versions in your user's home directory.

The Local Server: Simulating the Real World

Your PHP code needs a web server like Nginx or Apache to interpret the code and serve the resulting HTML to a browser. While you could install and configure these servers manually, this process can be complex and tedious. Fortunately, there are much better solutions for creating a local development server environment.

For the simplest of tasks, PHP comes with its own built-in web server. You can navigate to your project's public directory in a terminal and start it with a single command: `php -S localhost:8000`. This is incredibly handy for quickly testing a single script or running a small project without the need for any complex configuration. However, it's important to understand its limitations. The built-in server is single-threaded, meaning it can only handle one request at a time, and it's not designed to mimic the configuration or performance of a production server. It's a great tool for a quick preview, but not for serious development.

For a more professional and robust setup, the modern standard is to use containerization, and the undisputed king of containerization is Docker. Docker allows you to package your application and all its dependencies—including the web server, the exact version of PHP you need, and your database—into isolated, lightweight environments called containers. This approach solves the "it works on my machine" problem once and for all, because you can develop inside a container that is a perfect replica of the production environment. We will dive deep into creating your own Docker containers in Chapter 18, but for setting up a development environment, you can often leverage pre-built solutions.

Projects like Laravel Sail, for example, provide a command-line interface for managing a simple Docker development environment for Laravel applications. Even if you're not using Laravel, you can use a tool called Docker Compose to define all the services your application needs (a PHP container, an Nginx container, a MySQL container, etc.) in a single configuration file. With one command, `docker-compose up`, you can spin up your entire, isolated development environment. While there is a learning curve to Docker, the consistency and reproducibility it provides are invaluable for professional development.

For developers who find a full Docker setup intimidating or overly complex for their needs, there are excellent middle-ground solutions. On macOS, Laravel Valet is a popular choice. It configures Nginx to run in the background on your Mac and will automatically serve any PHP project you place within a designated directory, even providing local SSL certificates with minimal fuss. It's incredibly fast and uses very little RAM. The equivalent for Windows users is Laragon, which provides a similar, easy-to-use experience with an Nginx or Apache server, easy PHP version switching, and database management. These tools offer a significant step up from the built-in server without the full complexity of Docker.

Essential Command-Line Companions

A modern PHP developer lives and breathes on the command line. It's the most efficient way to interact with the ecosystem of tools that support the development process. A few of these tools are so fundamental that they are considered non-negotiable for any professional project.

First and foremost is Composer, the dependency manager for PHP. As we discussed in the previous chapter, Composer is the engine of the modern PHP ecosystem. It needs to be installed globally on your system so you can call it from any project directory. The installation is a straightforward process outlined on the official Composer website. Once installed, you should be able to run `composer --version` in your terminal and see it respond. We will explore Composer's full power in Chapter 5.

The second indispensable tool is Git. Git is a version control system that tracks every change you make to your code. It's like an infinite "undo" button for your entire project. It allows you to create branches to work on new features in isolation, and it's the foundation for collaborating with other developers. If you make a mistake, you can easily revert to a previous working state. Every professional developer must be proficient with Git. It's typically installed via the same package managers used for PHP (Homebrew, apt, etc.), and once installed, you should perform a one-time configuration with your name and email:

```
git config --global user.name "Your Name"

git config --global user.email
"youremail@example.com"
```

Finally, you will need a JavaScript runtime environment, which almost always means Node.js, along with its package manager, npm. You might be wondering why a PHP developer needs JavaScript tools. The reality of modern web development is that most applications have a frontend component that relies heavily on JavaScript and CSS. Tools for compiling, optimizing, and bundling these frontend assets, which we will cover in Chapter 21, are almost all built on top of Node.js. Installing Node.js is best done using a version manager like NVM (Node Version Manager), which allows you to install and switch between different Node versions, just as we do for PHP.

The Power of Debugging

One of the most significant leaps a developer can make in their journey is moving from "debugging" with `print` statements to using a proper step debugger. Sprinkling your code with `var_dump($variable); die();` is the programming equivalent of poking a machine with a stick to see what happens. It's a crude, slow, and inefficient way to figure out what's going wrong. A step debugger, on the other hand, is like having a superpower. It allows you to pause the execution of your code at any point, inspect the state of all variables, and then step through the code line by line to watch exactly how your application behaves.

The standard debugger for PHP is Xdebug. Setting it up involves three steps. First, you need to install the Xdebug extension for your version of PHP. This is usually done with a package manager like PECL (`pecl install xdebug`) or by installing a pre-packaged version (e.g., `brew install php-xdebug`). Second, you need to enable it in your `php.ini` configuration file. The exact location of this file can be found by running `php --ini`. You'll need to add a few lines to the file to enable Xdebug's step debugging mode:

```
[xdebug]

zend_extension=xdebug.so

xdebug.mode=debug

xdebug.start_with_request=yes
```

The final step is to configure your code editor to listen for connections from Xdebug. In VS Code, this is done with the *PHP Debug* extension. In PhpStorm, the debugger is built-in. You'll set a "breakpoint" in your code by clicking in the gutter next to a line number. This tells Xdebug, "Pause execution right here." Then, when you load the page in your browser (often with a helper browser extension to activate the debugger), your editor will pop to the front, and you'll be able to see the value of every variable in the current scope. You can then execute the next line, step into a function call to see what happens inside it, or just let the script continue running. Learning to use a step debugger is a non-negotiable skill that will save you countless hours of frustration and make you a vastly more effective developer.

Managing Your Database

Most web applications need to store data, which means you'll need a database server. The most common choices in the PHP world are MySQL (or its popular fork, MariaDB) and PostgreSQL. If you're using a Docker-based environment, you will simply add a container for your chosen database to your Docker Compose configuration. Tools like Laragon and Valet often include a database server as part of their standard installation.

Interacting with your database directly from the command line is possible, but it can be cumbersome. A graphical user interface (GUI) tool makes viewing data, designing table structures, and running ad-hoc queries much easier. There are many excellent, cross-platform options available. TablePlus is a popular, modern, and beautifully designed client that supports a wide range of databases. DBeaver is a powerful, free, and open-source universal database tool that is also very popular. If you use PhpStorm, it comes with a comprehensive and highly capable database client built directly into the IDE, allowing you to manage your database without ever switching windows. Choosing a GUI tool is a matter of personal preference, but having one in your toolkit is essential for efficient database management. With this final piece in place, your professional PHP workshop is now complete and ready for action.

CHAPTER THREE: PHP 8+ Fundamentals: A Modern Approach

With our development environment assembled, it's time to get our hands dirty and write some code. This chapter is your foundation in the PHP language as it exists today. We will not dwell on the historical baggage or the "old ways" of doing things. Instead, we'll start from a modern baseline, focusing on the syntax, features, and best practices that define professional PHP development in 2025 and beyond. Whether you're a complete newcomer or an experienced developer updating your skills, this chapter will ensure the fundamentals you learn are the right ones for building robust, readable, and maintainable applications. Our journey begins with the absolute basics, but we will quickly introduce the powerful features that make modern PHP a pleasure to work with.

The First Lines: Variables, Data Types, and Comments

At its core, every program manipulates data. In PHP, we store data in variables. A variable is simply a named container for a value. All variables in PHP are denoted by a leading dollar sign ($). They are case-sensitive and must start with a letter or an underscore, followed by any number of letters, numbers, or underscores. Let's look at a few examples:

```php
<?php


$name = "Alice"; // A string

$age = 30; // An integer

$price = 19.99; // A floating-point number

$is_active = true; // A boolean
```

```php
$user = null; // A special value
representing "no value"
```

In the code above, we've assigned values of different types to our variables. PHP is a dynamically typed language by default, which means you don't have to declare the type of a variable before you use it; the language figures it out at runtime. We see a few of PHP's primitive, or scalar, data types here: `string` (a sequence of characters), `int` (a whole number), `float` (a number with a decimal point), and `bool` (either `true` or `false`). We also see the special `null` type, which is used to explicitly represent the absence of a value.

You'll also notice the comments, which are lines starting with `//`. The PHP interpreter ignores these. They are for us, the human developers, to leave notes and explain what our code is doing. For multi-line comments, you can use / *to start and* / to end.

```php
<?php



/*

This is a multi-line comment.

It can span several lines and is useful for

more detailed explanations.

*/

$status = "pending"; // This is a single-
line comment.
```

Writing clear comments is a good habit, but the goal of modern PHP is to write code that is so clear and self-explanatory that it barely needs them. We'll see how features like strong typing and descriptive naming help us achieve this.

A New Era of Type Safety

While PHP's dynamic typing can be convenient for small scripts, it can become a significant source of bugs in large applications. A function might expect a number but receive a string, leading to unexpected behavior. Modern PHP solves this problem with a robust, optional type system. You can provide "type declarations" (also called type hints) for function arguments, return values, and class properties. This allows PHP to catch type-related errors early and helps you write more predictable and self-documenting code.

To get the full benefit of the type system, the very first line in your PHP files should be a special declaration: `declare(strict_types=1);`.

```php
<?php


declare(strict_types=1);



// The rest of your PHP code goes here.
```

This directive instructs PHP to enforce strict type checking. Without it, PHP will try to "coerce" types when possible. For example, if a function expects an `int` and you pass it the string `"5"`, PHP in its default "weak" mode will convert the string to an integer and proceed. In strict mode, it will throw a `TypeError`. For building robust applications, strict mode is the only way to go. It forces you to be explicit and intentional about the data you are working with.

Let's see this in action with a function. Here, we declare that the function `add` must be given two integers (`int`) as arguments, and that it must return an integer.

```php
<?php



declare(strict_types=1);



function add(int $a, int $b): int

{

    return $a + $b;

}



$result = add(5, 10); // This works
perfectly. $result is 15.

// $invalid = add(5, "10"); // This would
throw a TypeError in strict mode.
```

This simple addition makes our code significantly more robust. Your code editor can now immediately tell you if you're trying to pass the wrong type of data to a function, and the PHP engine itself provides a safety net.

PHP 8 introduced Union Types, which allow you to specify that a variable can be one of several different types. You declare this using a single pipe (|) between the types. This is incredibly useful for functions that can gracefully handle more than one kind of input.

```php
<?php



declare(strict_types=1);



function format_id(int|string $id): string

{

    // This function can accept either an
integer or a string.

    return "item-" . $id;

}



echo format_id(123); // Outputs "item-123"

echo format_id("abc"); // Outputs "item-abc"
```

The type system is a cornerstone of modern PHP development. It bridges the gap between the flexibility of a dynamic language and the safety of a statically typed one, giving you the best of both worlds.

Operators for the Modern Developer

Operators are the symbols we use to perform operations on variables and values. You're already familiar with the basics, such as the arithmetic operators (+, −, *, /, % for modulus) and the assignment operator (=). Comparison operators (==, !=, <, >) are used to compare values. It's crucial in modern PHP to almost always use the strict comparison operators: === (equal value and equal type) and !== (not equal value or not equal type). This avoids subtle bugs that can arise from type coercion with the loose == operator.

Modern PHP has also introduced several powerful operators designed to make common tasks more concise and less error-prone, especially when dealing with values that might be null.

The Null Coalescing Operator (??), introduced in PHP 7, provides a clean way to handle default values. It checks if a value is null and, if it is, provides a fallback. Before this operator, you would need to use a ternary statement with isset(), which was much more verbose.

```php
<?php



// The old way

$username = isset($_GET['user']) ?
$_GET['user'] : 'guest';



// The modern way with the null coalescing
operator
```

```php
$username = $_GET['user'] ?? 'guest';
```

```php
// It can even be chained

$name = $user_profile['name'] ??
$user_account['name'] ?? 'Anonymous';
```

This operator is a simple but significant quality-of-life improvement. It makes your intent clearer and your code cleaner.

Building on this, PHP 8 introduced the Nullsafe Operator (?->). This operator is a lifesaver when you need to chain method or property calls on an object that might be null. In the past, trying to call a method on a null object would immediately crash your script with a fatal error. You had to write cumbersome nested if statements to check if each part of the chain was not null. The nullsafe operator short-circuits the entire chain if it encounters a null value, returning null for the whole expression.

```php
<?php
```

```php
// Imagine we have a $session object that
might have a user, who might have a profile.

// The old, painful way:

if ($session !== null) {

    $user = $session->getUser();

    if ($user !== null) {
```

```php
    $profile = $user->getProfile();

    if ($profile !== null) {

        $avatar = $profile-
>getAvatarUrl();

    } else {

        $avatar = 'default.png';

    }

    } else {

        $avatar = 'default.png';

    }

} else {

    $avatar = 'default.png';

}


// The modern, elegant way with the nullsafe
and null coalescing operators:

$avatar = $session?->getUser()?-
>getProfile()?->getAvatarUrl() ??
'default.png';
```

The difference is night and day. A seven-line nested conditional block is reduced to a single, highly readable line of code. This is a perfect example of how modern PHP helps you write safer, more expressive code.

Controlling the Flow of Your Application

Control structures are the logical building blocks of your application. They allow you to execute different pieces of code based on certain conditions or to repeat an action multiple times. The fundamentals here have remained largely the same for a long time. The if, elseif, and else statements are used for conditional logic.

```php
<?php


$role = 'editor';


if ($role === 'admin') {

    echo 'Full access granted.';

} elseif ($role === 'editor') {

    echo 'Can write and edit content.';

} else {

    echo 'Read-only access.';

}
```

For repetitive tasks, we have loops. A `for` loop is great when you know exactly how many times you need to iterate. A `while` loop continues as long as a condition is true. But by far the most common and useful loop for web development is the `foreach` loop, which is designed to iterate over the elements of an array.

```php
<?php


$colors = ['red', 'green', 'blue'];


foreach ($colors as $color) {

    echo $color . "\n";

}



// You can also get the key (or index)

$user = ['name' => 'Bob', 'email' =>
'bob@example.com'];


foreach ($user as $key => $value) {

    echo "{$key}: {$value}\n";

}
```

While the `switch` statement has been a part of PHP for a long time, PHP 8 introduced a much more powerful and safer alternative: the `match` expression. A `match` expression is similar to `switch`, but with some key improvements. First, it uses strict comparison (===) instead of loose comparison (==), which eliminates a whole class of potential bugs. Second, a `match` expression is an expression, meaning it returns a value that can be assigned to a variable. Finally, it's more concise and requires that all possible conditions are handled (or a default case is provided), making your code more robust.

```php
<?php



$http_status_code = 200;



// The old switch statement

switch ($http_status_code) {

    case 200:

        $message = 'OK';

        break;

    case 404:

        $message = 'Not Found';

        break;

    case 500:

        $message = 'Internal Server Error';
```

```
        break;

    default:

        $message = 'Unknown status code';

        break;

}


// The new, improved match expression

$message = match ($http_status_code) {

    200 => 'OK',

    404 => 'Not Found',

    500 => 'Internal Server Error',

    default => 'Unknown status code',

};


echo $message; // Outputs 'OK'
```

The match expression is cleaner, safer, and more expressive. For any new code you write, you should prefer match over switch wherever possible.

Functions: Reusable Blocks of Code

Functions allow you to package a piece of logic into a reusable block. You can then "call" that function whenever you need to perform that specific task. We've already seen how to define a function with type declarations for its parameters and return value. A key concept with functions is variable scope. Variables defined inside a function are local to that function and cannot be accessed from the outside. Similarly, a function generally cannot access variables from the outside unless they are explicitly passed in as arguments.

```php
<?php

declare(strict_types=1);

$global_message = "Hello"; // Global scope

function greet(string $name): string
{
    $local_message = "Welcome"; // Local scope

    // echo $global_message; // This would cause an error

    return "{$local_message}, {$name}!";
}

echo greet("Alice");
```

```
// echo $local_message; // This would also
cause an error
```

PHP 7.4 introduced Arrow Functions, which provide a highly concise, single-line syntax for defining simple functions. They are particularly useful for callback functions used in array operations. Arrow functions automatically have access to variables from the parent scope, which eliminates the need for the use keyword that was required with traditional anonymous functions.

```php
<?php


$numbers =;

$multiplier = 10;


// Using a traditional anonymous function

$multiplied_old = array_map(function ($n)
use ($multiplier) {

    return $n * $multiplier;

}, $numbers);


// Using a modern arrow function

$multiplied_new = array_map(fn($n) => $n *
$multiplier, $numbers);
```

```
// Both variables now hold the array
```

Another major improvement, introduced in PHP 8, is Named
Arguments. Previously, you had to pass arguments to a function in
the exact order they were defined. If a function had many
parameters, especially optional ones, this could be confusing. With
named arguments, you can specify which parameter you are
providing the value for by using its name, allowing you to pass
them in any order and skip optional parameters more easily. This
makes your function calls self-documenting.

```php
<?php


function create_user(

    string $username,

    string $email,

    bool $is_admin = false,

    bool $send_welcome_email = true

) {

    // ... logic to create a user

}
```

```
// The old way - what does 'false' mean
here?

create_user('bob', 'bob@example.com', false,
true);



// The modern way with named arguments -
much clearer!

create_user(

    username: 'bob',

    email: 'bob@example.com',

    send_welcome_email: true

); // We can skip the optional $is_admin
parameter
```

Named arguments make your code significantly more readable, especially when calling functions with multiple boolean flags or optional settings.

Working with Collections: Modern Arrays

Arrays are one of the most fundamental data structures in PHP. They are incredibly versatile and can be used as a simple list, a dictionary (or hash map), a multi-dimensional matrix, and more. Modern PHP uses a short array syntax, [], which is cleaner than the older array() construct.

There are two main types of arrays. Indexed arrays use numeric keys, usually starting from 0. Associative arrays use named, string keys, which allows you to create more descriptive data structures.

```php
<?php


// An indexed array (a list of posts)

$posts = ['First Post', 'Second Post',
'Third Post'];

echo $posts; // Outputs 'Second Post'


// An associative array (a user record)

$user = [

    'id' => 123,

    'name' => 'Carol',

    'email' => 'carol@example.com',

];

echo $user['email']; // Outputs
'carol@example.com'
```

Modern PHP also provides convenient syntax for working with arrays. You can "destructure" an array to easily assign its values to individual variables.

```php
<?php

$coordinates =;

// Destructuring an indexed array
[$x, $y] = $coordinates;
// Now $x is 100 and $y is 200

$user_data = ['name' => 'David', 'age' =>
42];

// Destructuring an associative array (keys
must match)
['name' => $name, 'age' => $age] =
$user_data;
// Now $name is 'David' and $age is 42
```

Another powerful tool is the spread operator (. . .). When used inside an array, it will unpack another array's elements into the new one. This provides an elegant way to merge or prepend arrays.

```php
<?php
```

```php
$defaults = ['theme' => 'dark', 'language'
=> 'en'];

$user_prefs = ['language' => 'fr',
'font_size' => 16];



// The user_prefs will overwrite the
defaults

$settings = [...$defaults, ...$user_prefs];

// $settings is now ['theme' => 'dark',
'language' => 'fr', 'font_size' => 16]



$first_half = ['a', 'b'];

$second_half = ['c', 'd'];

$all = [...$first_half, ...$second_half]; //
$all is ['a', 'b', 'c', 'd']
```

These modern array features help you write cleaner and more expressive code when you're manipulating collections of data.

Handling Errors Gracefully

Things will inevitably go wrong in any application. A database might be unavailable, a third-party API might be down, or a user might provide invalid input. How your application handles these errors is a mark of its quality. The modern approach to error handling in PHP is to use exceptions. An exception is an object that is "thrown" when an error occurs. You can then "catch" this exception in a block of code and handle it gracefully, perhaps by logging the error and showing a user-friendly message.

This is done using a try...catch block. You place the code that might cause an error inside the try block. If an exception is thrown, the execution of the try block is immediately stopped, and the code inside the corresponding catch block is executed.

```php
<?php



declare(strict_types=1);



function calculate_inverse(float $number):
float

{

    if ($number === 0.0) {

        // Throwing an exception when
something goes wrong

        throw new
InvalidArgumentException('Cannot divide by
zero.');

    }

    return 1 / $number;

}
```

```php
try {

    $result1 = calculate_inverse(10); //
This works

    echo "Inverse of 10 is {$result1}\n";


    $result2 = calculate_inverse(0); // This
throws the exception

    echo "This line will never be
reached.\n";


} catch (InvalidArgumentException $e) {

    // This block runs because we caught the
exception

    echo "Caught an error: " . $e-
>getMessage() . "\n";

}


echo "Execution continues after the try-
catch block.";
```

This is a much cleaner and more reliable way to handle errors than the older PHP style of checking for `false` or `null` return values. All modern PHP libraries and frameworks use exceptions to signal errors, and you should too. Starting in PHP 7, both traditional errors and exceptions implement the same base `Throwable` interface, unifying the error handling model. Mastering these fundamental building blocks is the first and most important step in your journey. You now have a solid grasp of modern PHP syntax, its powerful type system, and the elegant operators and control structures that will form the basis of everything we build from here on.

CHAPTER FOUR: Advanced Object-Oriented Programming and Design Patterns

In the previous chapter, we established the fundamental syntax and structures of the PHP language. Now, we move from writing scripts to architecting applications. This leap requires a shift in thinking, from a procedural approach—a linear series of instructions—to an object-oriented one. Object-Oriented Programming (OOP) is not merely a set of language features; it's a paradigm for organizing complex systems into logical, reusable, and understandable components. It's the architectural blueprint for virtually every modern PHP framework and application. In this chapter, we will dissect the core principles of OOP and then explore how these principles are assembled into proven solutions known as design patterns. This is where you transition from being a coder to being a software engineer.

The Four Pillars of OOP

Object-Oriented Programming is built upon four foundational concepts that work in concert to create robust and flexible software: Encapsulation, Inheritance, Polymorphism, and Abstraction. Understanding these pillars is essential, as they provide the vocabulary and the mental model for designing complex systems. They are the rules of grammar that allow us to construct elegant and meaningful applications.

Encapsulation: The Protective Barrier

Encapsulation is the practice of bundling an object's data (its properties) and the methods that operate on that data into a single unit, a `class`. Crucially, it also involves hiding the internal state of the object from the outside world. Think of a car. You, the driver, interact with it through a simple interface: a steering wheel, pedals, and a gear stick. You don't need to know about the intricate details of the internal combustion engine, the fuel injection system, or the transmission. The car's complex inner workings are encapsulated, and you are protected from them (and they are protected from you).

In PHP, we achieve this using visibility keywords: `public`, `protected`, and `private`.

- `public`: A public property or method can be accessed from anywhere—outside the class, by the class itself, and by any child classes. This is the "steering wheel" of your object, the intended public interface.

- `private`: A private property or method can *only* be accessed from within the class that defined it. It cannot be accessed by child classes or from outside the class. This is the core of encapsulation, protecting the object's internal state.

- `protected`: A protected property or method can be accessed from within the class itself and by any classes that inherit from it. It remains hidden from the outside world. This is useful for providing internal tools for child classes to use.

Let's model a simple `BankAccount`.

```php
<?php

declare(strict_types=1);


class BankAccount

{

    private float $balance;
```

```php
    public function __construct(float
$startingBalance)

    {

        if ($startingBalance < 0) {

            throw new
InvalidArgumentException('Balance cannot be
negative.');

        }

        $this->balance = $startingBalance;

    }


    public function deposit(float $amount):
void

    {

        if ($amount <= 0) {

            throw new
InvalidArgumentException('Deposit amount
must be positive.');

        }

        $this->balance += $amount;

    }
```

```php
    public function withdraw(float $amount):
void

    {

        if ($amount <= 0) {

            throw new
InvalidArgumentException('Withdrawal amount
must be positive.');

        }

        if ($this->balance < $amount) {

            throw new
RuntimeException('Insufficient funds.');

        }

        $this->balance -= $amount;

    }


    public function getBalance(): float

    {

        return $this->balance;

    }

}
```

```php
$account = new BankAccount(100.0);

$account->deposit(50.0);

// $account->balance = 1000000; // FATAL
ERROR! Cannot access private property.

echo $account->getBalance(); // Outputs
150.0
```

By making the $balance property private, we prevent
outside code from setting it to an invalid state (like a negative
number, or a million dollars out of thin air). The only way to
modify the balance is through the public methods deposit()
and withdraw(), which contain the business logic to ensure the
transactions are valid. This principle of protecting an object's state
and controlling access through public methods is the essence of
encapsulation.

Inheritance: Building on What Exists

Inheritance allows a new class (the child or subclass) to be based
on an existing class (the parent or superclass). The child class
inherits all the public and protected properties and methods
from the parent, allowing you to reuse code and establish a logical
hierarchy. This models an "is-a" relationship. For example, a
SavingsAccount *is a* type of BankAccount.

We use the extends keyword to establish this relationship. The
child class can add its own new properties and methods, and it can
also override parent methods to provide a more specific
implementation.

```php
<?php
```

```php
class SavingsAccount extends BankAccount

{

    private float $interestRate;


    public function __construct(float
$startingBalance, float $interestRate)

    {


parent::__construct($startingBalance); //
Call the parent constructor

        $this->interestRate = $interestRate;

    }


    public function addInterest(): void

    {

        $interest = $this->getBalance() *
$this->interestRate;

        $this->deposit($interest); //
Reusing the parent's deposit method

    }

}
```

```php
$savings = new SavingsAccount(1000.0, 0.05);

$savings->addInterest();

echo $savings->getBalance(); // Outputs
1050.0
```

Here, `SavingsAccount` inherits the `deposit()`, `withdraw()`, and `getBalance()` methods from `BankAccount` without having to redefine them. We use `parent::__construct()` to ensure the parent class's setup logic is executed. Inheritance is a powerful tool for code reuse, but it should be used judiciously. Overusing it can lead to rigid, complex hierarchies that are difficult to change. Sometimes, composition (building objects out of other objects) is a more flexible approach.

Abstraction and Polymorphism: A Common Language

Abstraction is about hiding complexity and showing only the essential features of an object. Inheritance is one form of abstraction, but PHP provides two more explicit tools for this: `abstract` classes and `interfaces`.

An `interface` is a pure contract. It defines a set of `public` methods that a class *must* implement. It does not provide any implementation itself; it only dictates the "what," not the "how." This creates a "can-do" relationship. For example, anything that can be downloaded `can-do` the actions defined in a `Downloadable` interface.

```php
<?php



interface Downloadable
```

```
{

    public function getDownloadUrl():
string;

    public function getFileSize(): int; //
in bytes

}


class Ebook implements Downloadable

{

    // ... Ebook properties

    public function getDownloadUrl(): string

    {

        // ... logic to get URL

        return
"https://example.com/books/my-book.pdf";

    }


    public function getFileSize(): int

    {

        return 1500000;

    }
```

```
}


class SoftwarePatch implements Downloadable

{

    // ... Patch properties

    public function getDownloadUrl(): string

    {

        // ... logic to get URL

        return
"https://example.com/patches/patch-1.2.zip";

    }


    public function getFileSize(): int

    {

        return 5000000;

    }

}
```

This leads directly to polymorphism, which means "many forms." It is the ability to treat objects of different classes as if they were objects of a common superclass or interface. Because both Ebook and SoftwarePatch implement the Downloadable interface, we can write code that operates on *any* Downloadable object without needing to know its specific type.

```php
<?php


function startDownload(Downloadable $item):
void

{

    echo "Starting download from: " . $item->getDownloadUrl() . "\n";

    echo "File size: " . $item->getFileSize() . " bytes\n";

    // ... logic to perform the download

}


$book = new Ebook();

$patch = new SoftwarePatch();


startDownload($book);

startDownload($patch);
```

Our startDownload function is decoupled from the concrete classes. It can work with Ebooks, SoftwarePatches, or any other class we create in the future that implements

`Downloadable`. This makes our code incredibly flexible and extensible.

An `abstract class`, on the other hand, is a hybrid between an interface and a regular class. It cannot be instantiated on its own. It can contain both regular methods with implementations and `abstract` methods, which are like interface methods—they have no implementation and must be defined by the child class. Abstract classes are best used when you want to provide some common, shared functionality for a group of related subclasses while still forcing them to provide their own specific implementations for other parts.

Modern OOP Features in PHP 8+

PHP's object model has evolved significantly, with recent versions adding features that reduce boilerplate and enhance the language's expressive power.

Constructor Property Promotion

PHP 8.0 introduced a beautifully concise syntax for the common pattern of assigning constructor arguments to class properties. This feature, called constructor property promotion, dramatically cleans up your classes.

```php
<?php



// The old way (before PHP 8.0)

class UserProfile

{

    private string $bio;
```

```php
    private string $location;


    public function __construct(string $bio,
string $location)

    {

        $this->bio = $bio;

        $this->location = $location;

    }

}



// The modern way with constructor property
promotion

class UserProfileModern

{

    public function __construct(

        private string $bio,

        private string $location,

    ) {}

}
```

By simply adding a visibility keyword (public, protected, or private) to the constructor arguments, PHP automatically

58

creates the corresponding properties and assigns the values. The result is identical, but the code is far less redundant.

Readonly Properties and Immutable Objects

PHP 8.1 introduced `readonly` properties. A readonly property can only be initialized once, either from within the constructor or via a default value, and cannot be changed afterward. This is a powerful tool for creating immutable objects, also known as Value Objects. An immutable object's state cannot be modified after it's created, which makes your application's state more predictable and eliminates a whole class of bugs related to unexpected state changes.

```php
<?php


class Money
{
    public function __construct(
        public readonly float $amount,
        public readonly string $currency,
    ) {}
}


$price = new Money(19.99, 'USD');

// $price->currency = 'EUR'; // FATAL ERROR!
Cannot modify readonly property.
```

If you needed to represent a different price, you would create a new `Money` object instead of modifying the existing one. This pattern is fundamental to building predictable and robust systems.

Enumerations (Enums)

Another major addition in PHP 8.1 was first-class support for Enumerations, or Enums. An Enum is a type that has a fixed, limited number of possible values. Before Enums, developers would typically use a set of class constants for this purpose, but that approach was error-prone, as a function expecting one of those constants could be passed any arbitrary value. Enums solve this by creating a true type.

```php
<?php


enum UserStatus

{

    case Pending;

    case Active;

    case Suspended;

}


class User

{

    public UserStatus $status;

}
```

```php
function activateUser(User $user): void
{
    if ($user->status ===
UserStatus::Pending) {

        $user->status = UserStatus::Active;

        echo "User activated.\n";

    }

}


$user = new User();

$user->status = UserStatus::Pending;

activateUser($user);



// $user->status = 'active'; // This would
now cause a TypeError.
```

Enums can also have "backing" values (strings or ints) and methods, making them incredibly powerful for modeling states within an application.

Traits: Horizontal Code Reuse

PHP only allows a class to inherit from one parent (single inheritance). But what if you want to share a piece of functionality across several unrelated classes? This is where traits come in. A trait is a collection of methods that can be imported into a class using the use keyword. It provides a form of horizontal code reuse, modeling a "uses-a" or "has-a" relationship.

```php
<?php



trait Logger

{

    public function log(string $message):
void

    {

        // Imagine this writes to a file or
service

        echo "LOG: {$message}\n";

    }

}



class FileUploader

{

    use Logger;
```

```php
    public function upload(string
$filePath): void

    {

        // ... uploading logic ...

        $this->log("File {$filePath}
uploaded successfully.");

    }

}




class OrderProcessor

{

    use Logger;


    public function process(int $orderId):
void

    {

        // ... order processing logic ...

        $this->log("Order #{$orderId}
processed.");

    }

}
```

```
$uploader = new FileUploader();

$uploader->upload('document.pdf'); //
Outputs: LOG: File document.pdf uploaded
successfully.


$processor = new OrderProcessor();

$processor->process(123); // Outputs: LOG:
Order #123 processed.
```

Both `FileUploader` and `OrderProcessor` can now use the
`log()` method as if it were their own. Traits are an excellent tool
for sharing discrete units of functionality without being forced into
a rigid inheritance structure.

An Introduction to Design Patterns

As you build more complex applications, you'll start to notice
recurring problems. How do I create objects without coupling my
code to specific classes? How do I add new functionality to an
object without changing its code? How do I let objects
communicate without being tightly bound to each other?
Fortunately, developers have been solving these problems for
decades, and their solutions have been cataloged as **design
patterns**.

A design pattern isn't a specific piece of code you can copy and
paste. It is a general, reusable solution to a commonly occurring
problem within a given context. It's a template for how to solve a
problem that can be used in many different situations. Learning
patterns gives you a shared vocabulary with other developers and a
toolkit of proven architectural solutions.

Creational Patterns: Managing Object Creation

Creational patterns deal with the process of object creation, trying to create objects in a manner suitable to the situation.

The **Factory Method** pattern is one of the most common. It provides an interface for creating objects in a superclass but allows subclasses to alter the type of objects that will be created. This decouples your client code from the concrete classes it needs to instantiate.

```php
<?php



interface SocialMediaConnector

{

    public function post(string $message):
void;

}



class FacebookConnector implements
SocialMediaConnector { /* ... */ }

class TwitterConnector implements
SocialMediaConnector { /* ... */ }



abstract class SocialMediaProfile

{

    // The Factory Method
```

```php
    abstract protected function
createConnector(): SocialMediaConnector;



    public function publish(string
$message): void

    {

        $connector = $this-
>createConnector();

        $connector->post($message);

    }

}



class FacebookProfile extends
SocialMediaProfile

{

    protected function createConnector():
SocialMediaConnector

    {

        return new FacebookConnector();

    }

}
```

Now, the `publish` method doesn't know or care what kind of connector it's using; it just knows it gets an object that implements `SocialMediaConnector`.

Another core concept, closely related to creational patterns, is **Dependency Injection (DI)**. This principle states that an object should not create its own dependencies (the other objects it needs to work); they should be "injected" from an outside source. The most common form is constructor injection.

```php
<?php



// Bad: The class is tightly coupled to the
Logger

class ReportGenerator

{

    private Logger $logger;


    public function __construct()

    {

        $this->logger = new FileLogger(); //
Creates its own dependency

    }

}
```

```php
// Good: The class receives its dependency
(loose coupling)

class ReportGeneratorDI

{

    public function __construct(private
Logger $logger)

    {

        // The dependency is "injected"

    }

}



// The outside world is responsible for
creating the dependency

$logger = new FileLogger();

$reportGenerator = new
ReportGeneratorDI($logger);
```

This makes your code dramatically more flexible and, most importantly, testable. You can easily "inject" a fake or mock logger during testing. DI is the absolute bedrock of all modern PHP frameworks.

Structural Patterns: Composing Objects

Structural patterns explain how to assemble objects and classes into larger structures while keeping these structures flexible and efficient.

The **Adapter** pattern acts as a bridge between two incompatible interfaces. Imagine you have a new, third-party notification service you want to use, but its methods are different from the Notification interface your application expects. You can write an adapter.

```php
<?php



interface Notification

{

    public function send(string $title,
string $message): void;

}



class ThirdPartyNotifier

{

    public function broadcast(string
$jsonPayload): void { /* ... */ }

}



class NotifierAdapter implements
Notification

{

    public function __construct(private
ThirdPartyNotifier $notifier) {}
```

```php
    public function send(string $title,
string $message): void

    {

        $payload = json_encode(['title' =>
$title, 'alert' => $message]);

        $this->notifier-
>broadcast($payload);

    }

}
```

Your application can now work with the `NotifierAdapter` through its standard `Notification` interface, completely unaware of the `ThirdPartyNotifier` behind the scenes.

Behavioral Patterns: Managing Responsibilities

Behavioral patterns are concerned with algorithms and the assignment of responsibilities between objects.

The **Strategy** pattern is a classic example. It suggests you define a family of interchangeable algorithms and encapsulate each one in its own class. This allows the client to switch out the algorithm it uses at runtime. For example, an e-commerce checkout system could have different payment strategies.

```php
<?php



interface PaymentStrategy
```

```php
{
    public function pay(float $amount):
void;

}


class CreditCardPayment implements
PaymentStrategy { /* ... */ }

class PayPalPayment implements
PaymentStrategy { /* ... */ }


class ShoppingCart
{
    public function checkout(float $total,
PaymentStrategy $paymentMethod): void
    {
        // ...

        $paymentMethod->pay($total);
    }
}


$cart = new ShoppingCart();
```

```
$totalAmount = 250.00;

$paymentMethod = new CreditCardPayment(/*
... */);

$cart->checkout($totalAmount,
$paymentMethod);
```

If the user chose PayPal instead, you would simply instantiate and pass in a `PayPalPayment` object. The `ShoppingCart` remains unchanged, perfectly decoupled from the specific payment logic. These patterns are not just academic exercises; they are the tools you will use every day to write clean, maintainable, and scalable PHP applications.

CHAPTER FIVE: Dependency Management with Composer

If Object-Oriented Programming provides the architectural blueprints for a modern application, then Composer is the general contractor and logistics manager. It is the tool that sources, procures, and assembles all the prefabricated components—the third-party libraries—that our application will be built from. Before Composer arrived in 2012, the world of PHP development was a chaotic landscape of manual labor. If you wanted to use an external library, like a tool for sending emails or generating PDFs, you would embark on a tedious and error-prone journey. You would find the library's website, download a zip file, extract its contents into a folder in your project, and then begin the frustrating task of figuring out how to load its files using a long list of `require_once` statements. Updating that library was a nightmare you'd put off for as long as possible, and if two of your chosen libraries depended on different versions of a third library, you were in for a world of pain.

This ad-hoc approach made building complex applications brittle and difficult to maintain. It was the equivalent of constructing a skyscraper where every single beam, bolt, and window had to be custom-forged on-site. Composer changed everything. It introduced a standardized, automated, and reliable process for managing project dependencies. It is not an overstatement to say that Composer is the single most important tool in the modern PHP ecosystem. It transformed PHP development from a solitary craft into a collaborative engineering discipline, allowing us to stand on the shoulders of giants by seamlessly integrating the work of thousands of developers from around the world. Mastering Composer is not optional; it is the first and most critical step in building a professional PHP application.

The Core Components: `composer.json`, `composer.lock`, and the `vendor` Directory

At its heart, Composer operates on a few simple but powerful concepts. When you start a new project managed by Composer, you will find three key items at its root: a file named `composer.json`, a file named `composer.lock`, and a directory named `vendor`. Understanding the distinct role of each of these is fundamental to using the tool correctly.

The `composer.json` file is your project's manifest. It is a declaration of intent. In this file, you tell Composer what your project needs. You'll list the names of the libraries you want to use and, crucially, the version constraints you are willing to accept. For example, you might say, "I require a logging library, and I'm happy with any version that is at least 1.5 but less than version 2.0." This file is meant to be edited by you, the developer. It defines the direct dependencies of your project.

The `composer.lock` file is a record of what actually happened. After you tell Composer to install your dependencies, it goes out, finds all the packages you requested, and, just as importantly, all the packages *they* depend on (their "transitive dependencies"). It resolves all the version constraints to find a specific, compatible set of versions for every single library. It then records the exact versions it decided to install into the `composer.lock` file. This file is a snapshot, a precise manifest of every package and its exact version used in your project at a specific moment in time. You should almost never edit this file manually; it is managed by Composer itself.

Finally, the `vendor` directory is where the magic happens. This is the directory where Composer downloads the actual source code for all the libraries listed in the `composer.lock` file. It organizes them into a standardized directory structure and, most importantly, creates a single, powerful autoloader file. By including this one file in your application's startup process, you gain the ability to use any class from any of your installed libraries without ever writing another `require_once` statement. The `vendor` directory is disposable; if you delete it, you can perfectly recreate it at any time by running a single Composer command, which will read the `composer.lock` file and download the exact same versions of every package again.

Installing and Initializing a Project

Before you can use Composer, you need to install it on your system. Composer is a command-line tool written in PHP, and it's best installed globally so you can access it from any directory. The installation process is well-documented on the official Composer website, getcomposer.org, and typically involves downloading an installer script and running it with PHP. Once installed, you should be able to open your terminal and type `composer` to see a list of available commands.

Let's start a new project. Create a new directory and navigate into it. The first step is to create our `composer.json` file. While you can create this file manually, Composer provides a handy interactive command to get you started:

```
composer init
```

This command will ask you a series of questions about your project, such as the package name (in the format `vendor/project-name`), a description, the author, and the license. It will also ask if you want to define your dependencies interactively. For now, you can say no to these questions; we will add them later. Once you're done, you'll see a basic `composer.json` file has been created in your directory. It's a simple JSON object, and we will soon populate it with our requirements.

Managing Dependencies: `require`, `install`, and `update`

Now, let's add our first dependency. We need a logging library, and a very popular and well-respected one is Monolog. To add it to our project, we use the `require` command:

75

```
composer require monolog/monolog
```

A lot happens when you run this command. First, Composer connects to Packagist (the main Composer repository) to find information about the `monolog/monolog` package. It determines the latest stable version and adds a corresponding entry to your `composer.json` file. Then, it begins the "solving" process, figuring out which specific version of Monolog and any of its own dependencies it needs to install. Finally, it downloads the files into the `vendor` directory, creates or updates the `composer.lock` file with the exact versions it installed, and regenerates the autoloading files. Your project is now ready to use Monolog.

Now, imagine you push your project to a Git repository. A colleague clones it to their machine. Their project directory contains your `composer.json` and `composer.lock` files, but the `vendor` directory is empty (as it should be—we never commit the vendor directory to version control). To install all the project's dependencies, they will not run `composer require`. Instead, they will run:

```
composer install
```

This is a critical distinction. The `install` command does not look at `composer.json` to resolve versions. Instead, it looks directly at the `composer.lock` file. It will install the *exact* same versions of every single library that you had installed on your machine when you last updated the lock file. This guarantees that you, your colleague, your testing server, and your production server are all running the exact same code, eliminating a huge source of "it works on my machine" bugs. You should always run `composer install` when you first check out a project or after pulling in changes that include an updated `composer.lock` file.

So, when do you update your packages? Over time, the libraries you depend on will release new versions with bug fixes, security patches, and new features. To get these updates, you use the `update` command:

```
composer update
```

The `update` command looks at your `composer.json` file and the version constraints you've defined. It will find the latest possible versions that satisfy those constraints and install them. After it's done, it will write the new, updated versions into your `composer.lock` file. You would typically run this command periodically to keep your project up-to-date. If you only want to update a single package, you can specify it: `composer update monolog/monolog`. After running an update and testing that everything still works, you should commit the changed `composer.lock` file to your repository so that the rest of your team can get the new versions by running `composer install`.

Demystifying Version Constraints

The power and safety of Composer lie in its handling of package versions. When you specify a dependency, you also specify which versions of that dependency you are willing to accept. This is done using version constraints, and understanding them is crucial for maintaining a stable project. Most PHP libraries follow a standard called Semantic Versioning, or SemVer.

A SemVer version number is formatted as `MAJOR.MINOR.PATCH`, for example, `1.4.2`.

- **MAJOR** version changes (e.g., `1.4.2` to `2.0.0`) indicate incompatible API changes. Your code will likely break if you upgrade to a new major version without making changes.

- **MINOR** version changes (e.g., `1.4.2` to `1.5.0`) indicate new functionality has been added in a backward-compatible manner. You should be able to upgrade without anything breaking.

- **PATCH** version changes (e.g., 1.4.2 to 1.4.3) indicate backward-compatible bug fixes. These are always safe to apply.

When Composer adds a dependency for you, it typically uses the caret (^) operator. For example:

```
"monolog/monolog": "^3.5"
```

This is the most common and recommended constraint. The caret operator means you are willing to accept any new minor or patch releases, but not a new major release. In this case, it allows any version from 3.5.0 up to, but not including, 4.0.0. This gives you the best of both worlds: you get all the latest bug fixes and new features, but you are protected from backward-compatibility-breaking changes in the next major version.

Another common operator is the tilde (~). For example:

```
"monolog/monolog": "~3.5.0"
```

The tilde operator is a bit more restrictive. It says you are willing to accept new patch releases, but not new minor releases. In this case, it would allow any version from 3.5.0 up to, but not including, 3.6.0. This is useful if you are depending on a library that is known for being less stable and you want to be more cautious about new features.

You can also use comparison operators (>=, <, !=) and wildcards (3.5.*) to create more complex constraints, but the caret operator is the right choice for the vast majority of your dependencies. It provides a sensible balance between stability and staying up-to-date.

Autoloading with PSR-4

We've mentioned that Composer sets up an autoloader, but how does that actually work for our own application's code? The answer lies in the autoload section of composer.json and a community standard called PSR-4. PSR-4 is a specification that describes a standard way to map a class's namespace to its file path on the disk. By following this standard, we can tell Composer how to find and load our application's classes automatically.

Let's say we decide that all of our application's source code will live in a directory called src/ and all of our classes will be under the main namespace App. We would configure this in our composer.json like so:

```json
{

    "name": "my-app/cool-project",

    "require": {

        "monolog/monolog": "^3.5"

    },

    "autoload": {

        "psr-4": {

            "App\\": "src/"

        }

    }

}
```

The backslashes in the namespace need to be escaped with another backslash in JSON. This configuration tells Composer: "Any time you see a class that starts with the namespace App\, look for it inside the src/ directory."

So, if you have a class named App\Http\Controllers\UserController, Composer's autoloader will translate this into a file path. It takes the part of the class name that comes after the base namespace (`Http\Controllers\UserController`), replaces the namespace separators (`\`) with directory separators (`/`), and adds a `.php` extension. The final path it looks for is `src/Http/Controllers/UserController.php`.

After adding or changing the `autoload` section, you must tell Composer to regenerate its autoloader files. You can do this with the following command:

```
composer dump-autoload
```

This command doesn't download any packages; it simply re-scans your `composer.json` and the installed packages and rebuilds the optimized autoloader mapping. By adopting this PSR-4 convention, you create a clean, predictable structure for your project and completely eliminate the need for manual `require` statements.

Development Dependencies and Scripts

Not all of your project's dependencies are needed to make it run in production. You'll also have tools that you only use during development, such as testing frameworks, static analysis tools, and code style fixers. These are called development dependencies, and they should be listed in a separate section of your `composer.json` called `require-dev`.

The most popular testing framework for PHP is PHPUnit. To add it as a development dependency, you use the same `require` command but with a `--dev` flag:

```
composer require --dev phpunit/phpunit
```

This will add PHPUnit to the `require-dev` section. The primary difference is how Composer handles these packages based on the environment. When you run `composer install` or `composer update`, it installs all dependencies by default. However, when you deploy your application to a production server, you can tell Composer to skip the development packages to keep the installation lean and reduce the attack surface. This is done with a `--no-dev` flag:

```
composer install --no-dev --optimize-
autoloader
```

This command is standard practice for deployment scripts. It installs only the production dependencies from the lock file and runs an extra optimization step on the autoloader to make it as fast as possible for production traffic.

Composer also allows you to define custom commands and scripts in the `scripts` section of your `composer.json`. This is a convenient way to create shortcuts for common tasks. For example, you could configure it so that running `composer test` actually executes the PHPUnit test runner:

```
{

    "scripts": {

        "test": "phpunit",

        "cs-fix": "php-cs-fixer fix src",

        "analyse": "phpstan analyse src"

    }

}
```

Now, instead of having to remember the full command and path to the executable (which lives in `vendor/bin/`), any developer on the project can simply run `composer test`, `composer cs-fix`, or `composer analyse`. This creates a consistent and easy-to-use command interface for your project's quality assurance tools.

Best Practices and Workflow

To use Composer effectively and professionally, there are a few golden rules that you should always follow. These practices ensure your project remains stable, secure, and easy for other developers to work with.

First, **always commit your `composer.lock` file to version control**. This is the most important rule. The lock file is your guarantee of reproducibility. It ensures every single person and system running your application is using the exact same set of dependencies. Without it, running `composer install` on two different machines could result in different package versions being installed, leading to unpredictable behavior.

Second, **never commit the `vendor` directory to version control**. This directory can be easily and perfectly recreated from your `composer.lock` file. Committing it would add a massive amount of third-party code to your repository, making it bloated and slow. Add a line with `/vendor/` to your `.gitignore` file to ensure it's never accidentally committed.

Third, run `composer install` after checking out a project or pulling in changes from your team. This will sync your local `vendor` directory with the state defined in the `composer.lock` file.

Fourth, use `composer require` to add new dependencies. Don't edit `composer.json` manually and then run `update`, as this could unintentionally update other packages as well. The `require` command is more explicit and safer.

Finally, run `composer update` periodically to bring in the latest compatible versions of your dependencies. Do this as a deliberate action, not just randomly. After updating, run your test suite to ensure that the new package versions haven't introduced any regressions. Once you're confident everything is working, commit the updated `composer.lock` file. By integrating these practices into your daily workflow, you harness the full power of Composer to build robust, maintainable, and professional PHP applications.

CHAPTER SIX: Understanding MVC and Modern PHP Frameworks

We have journeyed through the core of the PHP language, learned how to structure code with object-oriented principles, and mastered the art of assembling our toolkit with Composer. We can now write clean, modern, and reusable PHP classes. But an application is more than just a collection of classes. As a project grows from a handful of files to hundreds or thousands, a new challenge emerges: chaos. Without a high-level plan, our beautifully crafted components can become entangled in a messy web of dependencies, creating what is often grimly referred to as a "big ball of mud." Modifying one part of the application causes unpredictable side effects in another, testing becomes a nightmare, and bringing new developers up to speed feels like handing them a map with no compass.

To conquer this complexity, we need an architectural blueprint. We need a proven strategy for organizing our code into distinct, manageable pieces with clearly defined roles and responsibilities. In the world of web development, the most influential and enduring of these blueprints is the Model-View-Controller (MVC) architectural pattern. It is the conceptual foundation upon which virtually every modern PHP framework is built. Understanding MVC is not just about learning an acronym; it's about learning a new way to think about the structure of your application. It's the mental framework that allows you to move from writing code to engineering software systems that are logical, maintainable, and scalable.

Deconstructing the Pattern: Model, View, and Controller

At its core, the MVC pattern is a strategy for separating concerns. It advocates for dividing an application into three interconnected but distinct components. Each component has a very specific job, and the pattern defines the rules for how they are allowed to communicate with each other. This separation is the key to managing complexity. By isolating different aspects of the application, we can work on them independently, test them more easily, and evolve them over time without breaking the entire system. Let's break down the role of each piece of the puzzle.

The Model: The Heart of the Application

The Model is the most important, and often the most misunderstood, part of the MVC triad. It is not, as many beginners assume, just the database table. The Model is the core of your application. It represents the business logic, the data, and the rules that govern your application's domain. If you were building an e-commerce application, your Model layer would contain objects representing Products, Orders, and Customers. It would also contain the logic for calculating shipping costs, applying discounts, and processing payments. The Model is the brain of the operation.

Critically, the Model should be completely unaware of how it is being presented or who is interacting with it. It knows nothing about HTML, HTTP, or web browsers. It could just as easily be used by a command-line tool, a mobile app's API, or a desktop application. This "framework agnosticism" is a key characteristic of a well-designed Model layer. It contains the pure, unadulterated logic of your business. This layer is often composed of several types of objects we touched upon in Chapter 4: Entities (objects with an identity, like a `User` with an ID), Value Objects (immutable objects defined by their attributes, like a `Money` object), and Services (objects that perform specific business operations, like a `PaymentProcessor`). The Model's job is to manage the state of the application and enforce its rules.

The View: The Face of the Application

If the Model is the brain, the View is the face. The View's sole responsibility is presentation. It takes the data prepared by the

Model and renders it into a format suitable for the user, which in our case is almost always HTML. The View should be as "dumb" as possible. This means it should contain the absolute minimum amount of logic. The logic within a View should be limited to simple presentation tasks: looping over a list of products to display them in a table, using an `if` statement to show or hide a "login" button, or formatting a date for display.

The View should never contain business logic. It should not perform database queries, calculate prices, or decide if a user has permission to see something. It receives a pre-packaged set of data and its only job is to make it look good. In modern PHP applications, the View is almost always implemented using a templating engine, a topic we will explore in depth in Chapter 11. These engines provide a simplified syntax for embedding presentation logic into an HTML template, which helps enforce the separation from the core application logic. By keeping the View layer dumb, we ensure that a change in design—like rebuilding the entire frontend with a new CSS framework—has zero impact on the underlying business logic in the Model.

The Controller: The Traffic Director

The Controller acts as the intermediary, the glue that connects the user's actions to the application's core logic. When a request arrives from a user's browser, it is the Controller's job to handle it. The Controller parses the incoming request, figures out what the user is trying to do, and then coordinates the necessary actions. It is the traffic director of the application.

A Controller's job is to receive input, interact with the Model, and select a View. For example, a `ProductController` might have a `show` method. This method would receive a product ID from the URL. It would then ask the Model, "Hey, can you find me the product with this ID?" The Model would do its work— finding the product in the database, checking inventory levels, etc.—and return a `Product` object. The Controller would then take that `Product` object, pass it to a specific View template (e.g., `product_details.html`), and instruct the View to render itself.

A well-designed Controller is thin. Like the View, it should not contain business logic. Its role is purely one of coordination and translation. It translates an incoming HTTP request into a method call on the Model and then translates the result from the Model into a response, usually by rendering a View. It ensures that the Model and the View never talk to each other directly, enforcing the separation that is so central to the MVC pattern.

Following the Flow: The Request Lifecycle

To make this all concrete, let's trace the journey of a single HTTP request through a typical MVC application. Imagine a user wants to view their profile page by navigating to the URL `https://example.com/user/123`.

1. **The Entry Point**: The request doesn't just magically find the right PHP file. All modern frameworks use a design pattern called the "Front Controller." This means that every single request, regardless of the URL, is directed by the web server to a single PHP file (often `public/index.php`). This file acts as the single entry point for the entire application. It boots up the framework, sets up the environment, and starts the process.

2. **Routing**: The framework's router is the first major component to inspect the request. The router's job is to look at the request's URI (`/user/123`) and the HTTP method (e.g., `GET`) and decide which piece of code should handle it. The router has a list of predefined routes, mapping URL patterns to specific Controller methods. In this case, it finds a route that matches `/user/{id}` and knows that this should be handled by the `show` method on the `UserController`. We will dive deep into routing in Chapter 8.

3. **Dispatching to the Controller**: The router then "dispatches" the request to the designated Controller method. It instantiates the `UserController` class and calls the `show()` method, passing the `{id}` from the URL (in this case, `123`) as an argument.

4. **Controller Interacts with the Model**: Now inside the `show(int $id)` method, the Controller gets to work. It does not query the database directly. Instead, it interacts with the Model layer. It might call a method on a `UserRepository` or `UserService` object, something like `$user = $userRepository->find($id);`. This is where Dependency Injection, which we discussed in Chapter 4, is crucial. The framework's service container will have automatically provided the `UserController` with the `UserRepository` instance it needs.

5. **Model Executes Business Logic**: The `UserRepository`'s `find()` method contains the logic for retrieving the user. It connects to the database, executes a query to find the user with an ID of 123, and then uses that data to create a `User` entity object. If the user doesn't exist, the Model might throw an exception. The Model then returns the fully populated `User` object back to the Controller.

6. **Controller Prepares and Selects the View**: The Controller now has the data it needs—the `User` object. It then decides which View to render. It calls the view layer, specifying the template file (e.g., `user/profile.php`) and passing it an array of data, like `['user' => $user]`.

7. **View Renders the Response**: The View layer now takes over. The `user/profile.php` template is executed. It receives the `user` variable and uses it to render the final HTML. It might contain code like `<h1><?= htmlspecialchars($user->getName())`

`?></h1>` and `<p>Email: <?=`
`htmlspecialchars($user->getEmail())`
`?></p>`. The View's job is simply to fill in the blanks in the template with the data it was given.

8. **Sending the Response**: Once the View has finished rendering the HTML, the result is captured into a `Response` object. This object, containing the final HTML content and HTTP headers (like the `200 OK` status code), is returned all the way back up the chain and sent back to the user's browser, which then displays the profile page.

This entire lifecycle demonstrates the clean separation of concerns. The router only cares about URLs. The Controller only cares about coordinating. The Model only cares about business data and rules. The View only cares about presentation. Each part has a clearly defined job, making the whole system easier to understand, debug, and maintain.

The Rise of Modern PHP Frameworks

The MVC pattern provides the blueprint, but building all the underlying components—the router, the front controller, the templating engine, the dependency injection container—from scratch for every project would be incredibly time-consuming. This is the problem that modern PHP frameworks solve. A framework is a skeleton application that provides all of this common "plumbing" and infrastructure out of the box, allowing you to focus on writing the code that is unique to your application: your specific Models, Views, and Controllers.

When you start a new project with a framework like Laravel or Symfony, you are not starting with a blank slate. You are starting with a well-organized directory structure that has dedicated places for your controllers, your models (often called entities), and your views (templates). The framework provides a powerful routing component, a sophisticated service container for managing dependencies, and integrations with database tools (ORMs) and templating engines. It has already implemented the front controller pattern and the entire request lifecycle for you.

These frameworks are the embodiment of the principles we've discussed. Laravel, known for its elegant syntax and developer-friendly features, provides the Blade templating engine for its View layer, the Eloquent ORM for its Model layer, and a clear structure for its Controllers and routing. Symfony, known for its flexibility and robust collection of reusable components, uses the Twig templating engine for its Views, the Doctrine ORM for its Models, and a powerful routing system to wire everything together. Both frameworks rely heavily on a service container to manage class dependencies, making it easy to follow the principles of Dependency Injection and write highly testable code.

While MVC is the conceptual ancestor, it's worth noting that the patterns in modern frameworks have evolved. You might hear terms like Model-View-Adapter, Action-Domain-Responder (ADR), or simply the "Request-Response" pattern. While the specifics differ, the core philosophy remains the same: separating the concerns of receiving a request, executing core business logic, and formatting a response. The fundamental division of responsibilities between routing, domain logic, and presentation is a constant. For all practical purposes, understanding the roles of the Model, View, and Controller gives you the essential mental model to be productive in any modern PHP framework. The framework simply provides a mature, battle-tested implementation of this pattern, saving you from reinventing the wheel and allowing you to get straight to building great applications.

CHAPTER SEVEN: Building a RESTful API with a Microframework

Having explored the high-level architecture of MVC, we are now equipped to build something tangible. While full-stack frameworks like Laravel and Symfony are powerhouses for building complex, feature-rich web applications, there is a growing demand for a different kind of application: the Application Programming Interface, or API. In the modern web, where frontend JavaScript frameworks and mobile applications often handle the presentation layer, the backend's primary role is frequently reduced to a lean, efficient data provider. This is the world of the API, and for this task, a different class of tool often shines: the microframework.

In this chapter, we will shift our focus from applications that serve HTML to applications that serve data. We will deconstruct the principles of REST (Representational State Transfer), the architectural style that underpins the vast majority of modern web APIs. We will then roll up our sleeves and use a popular PHP microframework to build a practical, working RESTful API from the ground up. This process will solidify your understanding of the request-response lifecycle and provide a foundational skill set for building the backend services that power today's interactive and distributed applications.

What Exactly is a RESTful API?

Before we can build one, we need to understand the terminology. An API is a contract, a set of rules and definitions that allows one piece of software to communicate with another. A web API is simply an API that does its communicating over the web, almost always using the HTTP protocol that powers your web browser. When you hear the term "RESTful API," it refers to a web API that is designed according to the principles of REST. REST isn't a strict protocol like SOAP or a specification like GraphQL; it's an architectural style, a set of constraints and best practices for creating scalable, maintainable, and easy-to-use web services.

These principles were defined by Roy Fielding in his doctoral dissertation in 2000, based on the very principles that made the World Wide Web itself so successful and scalable. The core idea of REST is to treat everything as a "resource." A resource is any piece of information that can be named: a user, a product, an order, a blog post. Each resource has a unique identifier, which in the context of a web API is its URL (Uniform Resource Locator).

To interact with these resources, a client (like a mobile app or a JavaScript frontend) sends an HTTP request to the resource's URL. The key insight of REST is to use the standard HTTP methods—the verbs of the web—to define the action you want to perform on that resource.

- GET: Retrieve a representation of a resource. (e.g., get details for a specific user). This is a safe and idempotent operation, meaning it can be called multiple times without changing anything.

- POST: Create a new resource. (e.g., create a new user). This is not idempotent, as calling it multiple times will create multiple new users.

- PUT: Update an existing resource completely. (e.g., replace an existing user's profile with a new one). This is idempotent.

- PATCH: Partially update an existing resource. (e.g., change only a user's email address). This is not necessarily idempotent.

- DELETE: Remove a resource. (e.g., delete a user). This is idempotent.

By leveraging these standard HTTP verbs, the API becomes predictable and intuitive. The URLs identify the "nouns" (the resources), and the HTTP methods identify the "verbs" (the actions). For example:

- `GET /users/123`: Retrieve user with ID 123.

- `DELETE /users/123`: Delete user with ID 123.

- `POST /users`: Create a new user.

Another critical principle of REST is that communication must be stateless. This means that every single request from a client to the server must contain all the information the server needs to understand and process the request. The server does not store any information about the client's session between requests. This constraint is what allows RESTful services to be incredibly scalable, as any request can be handled by any server, making it easy to add more servers to handle increased load.

Finally, when the server responds, it sends back a "representation" of the resource. In the early days of the web, this was almost always HTML. In the modern API world, the representation is almost universally JSON (JavaScript Object Notation), a lightweight, human-readable data format that is easy for virtually any programming language to parse. The response also includes a standard HTTP status code to indicate the outcome of the request (e.g., `200 OK`, `201 Created`, `404 Not Found`, `500 Internal Server Error`).

The Case for a Microframework

With a clear understanding of what we want to build, the next question is what tool to use. While a full-stack framework like Laravel could certainly do the job, it often brings along a lot of features we simply don't need for a pure API—templating engines, session management, form validation libraries, and so on. This is where microframeworks come in.

A microframework is a deliberately minimalist framework. It provides the bare essentials for building a web application or API and nothing more. At its core, a microframework typically provides two key pieces of functionality: a powerful router to map incoming requests to the correct code, and a convenient abstraction for handling the HTTP request and response objects. That's it. Anything else you need—a database library, a logging tool, an authentication component—is your responsibility to choose and integrate using Composer.

This philosophy offers several advantages for API development. First, it results in less overhead. Your application is leaner and faster because it only contains the code it absolutely needs. Second, it gives you, the developer, complete control. You are not bound by the conventions or choices of a large framework; you can choose the best tool for every job. This flexibility is perfect for building services that need to be highly specialized or integrate with unconventional data sources. For our purposes, it also serves as an excellent teaching tool. By building from a minimal base, you gain a much clearer understanding of how the fundamental components of a web application fit together, knowledge that is directly transferable to any other framework you might use in the future. For this chapter, we will use Slim, a popular and mature PHP microframework known for its simplicity and excellent documentation.

Laying the Foundation: Project Setup

Let's begin by creating our project. First, create a new directory for your API and navigate into it with your terminal. Our first step, as with any modern PHP project, is to initialize Composer.

```
composer init
```

You can accept the defaults for most of the questions. This command creates our composer.json file. Now, we'll use Composer to pull in our microframework and a necessary companion library. Slim, like many modern PHP frameworks, is built on the standards defined by the PHP-FIG. Specifically, it doesn't come with its own HTTP message implementation; instead, it requires any library that is compatible with the PSR-7 standard. Slim provides its own compatible library, which we will install alongside the framework itself.

```
composer require slim/slim slim/psr7
```

Composer will download these packages and their dependencies into the `vendor` directory and generate our `composer.lock` file and autoloader.

Next, we need to create a basic directory structure. A standard practice is to have a `public` directory that will be the "document root" for your web server. This is where the single front controller entry point will live. We'll also create a `src` directory for our application's source code, though we won't use it just yet.

```
mkdir public
```

```
mkdir src
```

Inside the `public` directory, create a file named `index.php`. This will be the Front Controller for our entire API. All incoming requests will be routed to this single file. Its job is to bootstrap the application and kick off the framework.

```php
<?php

// public/index.php


use Psr\Http\Message\ResponseInterface as
Response;

use Psr\Http\Message\ServerRequestInterface
as Request;

use Slim\Factory\AppFactory;


// 1. Require the Composer autoloader
```

```php
require __DIR__ . '/../vendor/autoload.php';


// 2. Instantiate the Slim App

$app = AppFactory::create();


// 3. Define our first route

$app->get('/', function (Request $request,
Response $response, $args) {

    $response->getBody()->write("Hello,
world!");

    return $response;

});


// 4. Run the application

$app->run();
```

To test this, we can use PHP's built-in web server. From your project's root directory, run the following command in your terminal:

```
php -S localhost:8080 -t public
```

This tells PHP to start a web server on port 8080 and to use the public directory as the document root. Now, if you open a new terminal window and use a tool like curl, or simply navigate to http://localhost:8080 in your web browser, you should see the text "Hello, world!". Our microframework is alive and handling requests.

From "Hello World" to "Hello JSON"

Our API needs to speak JSON, not plain text. Let's modify our first route to return a proper JSON response. The `Response` object provided to our route handler is a PSR-7 object. To modify it, we first get its body, write our content to it, and then return a new response object with the appropriate `Content-Type` header.

```php
<?php

// ... inside public/index.php



$app->get('/hello/{name}', function (Request $request, Response $response, array $args) {

    $name = $args['name'];

    $data = ['message' => "Hello, {$name}"];



    $payload = json_encode($data);



    $response->getBody()->write($payload);



    return $response

            ->withHeader('Content-Type', 'application/json');
```

```
});
```

We've done two new things here. First, we've added a placeholder, {name}, to our route's URL pattern. Slim automatically captures the value from the URL and provides it in the $args array. Second, after encoding our data array into a JSON string, we return the response while chaining the withHeader() method. This ensures the client knows it's receiving JSON data.

If you restart your server and make a request to http://localhost:8080/hello/Alice with curl, you'll see the difference:

```
curl -i http://localhost:8080/hello/Alice
```

```
HTTP/1.1 200 OK

Host: localhost:8080

Date: ...

Connection: close

X-Powered-By: PHP/8.3.4

Content-Type: application/json
```

```
{"message":"Hello, Alice"}
```

The -i flag tells curl to include the HTTP headers in the output. Notice that the Content-Type is now correctly set to application/json, and the body is a valid JSON object. We are now officially serving data.

Building a Resourceful API: A Task List

Let's build a more realistic API for managing a simple list of tasks. For now, we will store our tasks in a simple PHP array to keep the focus on the API logic itself. We will tackle persistent database storage in Chapter 9. Add this mock data at the top of your `public/index.php` file, after the `use` statements.

```php
<?php

// ...

$tasks = [

    ['id' => 1, 'title' => 'Learn RESTful APIs', 'completed' => true],

    ['id' => 2, 'title' => 'Build a microframework app', 'completed' => false],

    ['id' => 3, 'title' => 'Master modern PHP', 'completed' => false],

];
```

Now, let's implement the five standard endpoints for this resource.

GET /tasks: Listing all Resources

This endpoint should return the complete list of tasks. We'll define a new route and, to make our code reusable, let's also pass our `$tasks` array into the closure using the `use` keyword.

```php
<?php

// ...
```

```php
$app->get('/tasks', function (Request
$request, Response $response) use ($tasks) {

    $payload = json_encode($tasks);

    $response->getBody()->write($payload);

    return $response->withHeader('Content-
Type', 'application/json');

});
```

A request to GET http://localhost:8080/tasks will now return the full array of tasks as a JSON object.

GET /tasks/{id}: Retrieving a Single Resource

This endpoint needs to find a specific task by its ID. We'll get the ID from the URL, search our array, and handle the case where the task is not found.

```php
<?php

// ...



$app->get('/tasks/{id}', function (Request
$request, Response $response, array $args)
use ($tasks) {

    $taskId = (int) $args['id'];

    $task = null;
```

```php
    foreach ($tasks as $t) {

        if ($t['id'] === $taskId) {

            $task = $t;

            break;

        }

    }


    if ($task) {

        $payload = json_encode($task);

        $response->getBody()-
>write($payload);

        return $response-
>withHeader('Content-Type',
'application/json');

    }


    // Task not found, return a 404 response

    return $response->withStatus(404);

});
```

Here, if we find the task, we return it with a 200 OK status (which is the default). If the loop finishes and we haven't found a task, we return an empty response with a 404 Not Found status code. This is a crucial part of building a robust API: using the correct HTTP status codes to communicate outcomes.

POST `/tasks`: Creating a New Resource

To create a task, the client will send a POST request with the new task's data in the request body as a JSON object. Our handler needs to read this body, decode it, add a new task to our array, and then return the newly created task to the client.

```php
<?php

// ...



// IMPORTANT: We need to pass the tasks
array by reference (&) to modify it.

$app->post('/tasks', function (Request
$request, Response $response) use (&$tasks)
{

    // Get the JSON from the request body

    $body = $request->getBody()-
>getContents();

    $newTaskData = json_decode($body, true);



    // For simplicity, we'll just generate a
new ID.

    // In a real app, the database would
handle this.
```

```php
    $newId = max(array_column($tasks, 'id'))
+ 1;


    $newTask = [

        'id' => $newId,

        'title' => $newTaskData['title'] ??
'Untitled', // Basic validation/defaulting

        'completed' =>
$newTaskData['completed'] ?? false,

    ];


    $tasks[] = $newTask;


    $payload = json_encode($newTask);

    $response->getBody()->write($payload);


    // Return the response with a 201
Created status code

    return $response

        ->withHeader('Content-Type',
'application/json')

        ->withStatus(201);
```

```
});
```

There are two key things to note here. First, we passed $tasks by reference (use (&$tasks)) so that when we add a new item to the array, the change persists for subsequent requests (at least for as long as our development server is running). Second, upon success, we return a 201 Created status code. This is the correct semantic code for a successful resource creation.

You can test this with curl:

```
curl -X POST http://localhost:8080/tasks \

-H "Content-Type: application/json" \

-d '{"title": "Write chapter 7",
"completed": true}'
```

PUT /tasks/{id}: Updating a Resource

A PUT request is used to completely replace an existing resource. The client will send the full new representation of the task to the endpoint.

```php
<?php

// ...



$app->put('/tasks/{id}', function (Request
$request, Response $response, array $args)
use (&$tasks) {

    $taskId = (int) $args['id'];

    $body = $request->getBody()-
>getContents();
```

```php
$updatedData = json_decode($body, true);


$taskIndex = -1;

foreach ($tasks as $index => $t) {

    if ($t['id'] === $taskId) {

        $taskIndex = $index;

        break;

    }

}


if ($taskIndex === -1) {

    return $response->withStatus(404);
// Not Found

}


// Replace the old task with the new one

$tasks[$taskIndex] = [

    'id' => $taskId,

    'title' => $updatedData['title'],
```

```php
        'completed' =>
$updatedData['completed'],

    ];



    $payload =
json_encode($tasks[$taskIndex]);

    $response->getBody()->write($payload);

    return $response->withHeader('Content-
Type', 'application/json');

});
```

We find the index of the existing task, and if it exists, we replace the entire array element with the new data. A successful PUT request typically returns a 200 OK status.

DELETE /tasks/{id}: Deleting a Resource

Finally, the DELETE verb is used to remove a resource. This operation should be idempotent; deleting something that's already gone shouldn't cause an error.

```php
<?php

// ...



$app->delete('/tasks/{id}', function
(Request $request, Response $response, array
$args) use (&$tasks) {

    $taskId = (int) $args['id'];
```

```
// Find and remove the task

$tasks = array_filter($tasks, function
($task) use ($taskId) {

    return $task['id'] !== $taskId;

});



// The correct response for a successful
deletion is 204 No Content.

return $response->withStatus(204);

});
```

A successful DELETE request should return a 204 No
Content status code. This indicates to the client that the
operation was successful, and that there is no body content to parse
in the response.

We have now successfully built a complete, albeit simple,
RESTful API. We have endpoints for all five primary CRUD
(Create, Read, Update, Delete) operations, and we are using
standard HTTP methods and status codes to communicate clearly
and predictably. However, you may have noticed that our
index.php file is getting quite long and the closures are starting
to contain a fair bit of logic. This is a common growing pain.
While fine for a handful of routes, this approach doesn't scale well.
To create a more organized and maintainable structure, we need to
extract this logic into dedicated classes—Controllers—and explore
ways to handle common tasks like authentication and logging

across multiple routes using Middleware. These are precisely the topics we will tackle in the next chapter.

CHAPTER EIGHT: Routing, Middleware, and Controllers

In our last chapter, we successfully built a functioning RESTful API. We hammered together five endpoints that allowed a client to create, read, update, and delete tasks. It worked, and in doing so, it beautifully illustrated the core principles of REST and the elegant simplicity of a microframework. However, if you stepped back and looked at our handiwork—a single, ever-growing `index.php` file—a professional unease likely began to set in. All our application logic, from parsing requests to manipulating our in-memory "database," was crammed into a series of anonymous functions. This approach is perfectly fine for a handful of routes, but it is the programmatic equivalent of building a house without any interior walls. As soon as you want to add a second room or a third, you realize you have a scalability problem.

To build robust, professional applications, we need to partition our code. We need to move beyond simple closures and organize our logic into dedicated, reusable, and testable classes. This chapter is about building those interior walls. We will dismantle the monolithic structure of our `index.php` and refactor our logic into **Controllers**, classes designed specifically to handle groups of related requests. We will then tackle the challenge of handling common tasks that apply to many different requests—like logging, authentication, or error handling—by introducing **Middleware**, a powerful pattern for filtering and modifying requests and responses as they flow through the application. Finally, we'll see how routing ties these two concepts together, creating a clean, organized, and scalable application architecture.

From Closures to Classes: The Controller Pattern

The first and most important step in organizing our API is to extract the logic from our route closures into dedicated classes. A Controller is a class that groups together the logic for a set of

related resource endpoints. Instead of a closure for GET /tasks
and another for POST /tasks, we will have a single
TaskController class with methods like listAll() and
create(). This brings immediate and significant benefits. It
makes our code easier to find, read, and reason about. It allows us
to reuse helper methods within the same controller. Most
importantly, it makes our application logic testable in isolation,
away from the complexities of the web server and HTTP requests.

Let's begin the refactoring process. First, we need to tell Composer
how to find our new classes. We'll use the PSR-4 autoloading
standard we discussed in Chapter 5. Open your composer.json
file and add an autoload section to map the App namespace to
the src/ directory.

```json
{

    "require": {

        "slim/slim": "^4.12",

        "slim/psr7": "^1.6"

    },

    "autoload": {

        "psr-4": {

            "App\\": "src/"

        }

    }

}
```

After saving this change, you must run composer dump-autoload in your terminal to regenerate the autoloader files with this new mapping. Now, we can create our controller. Create a new directory structure src/Controllers/ and inside it, a new file named TaskController.php.

```php
<?php

// src/Controllers/TaskController.php


declare(strict_types=1);


namespace App\Controllers;


use Psr\Http\Message\ResponseInterface as Response;

use Psr\Http\Message\ServerRequestInterface as Request;


class TaskController

{

    // For now, we'll just move our mock data in here as a private property.

    private array $tasks = [

        ['id' => 1, 'title' => 'Learn RESTful APIs', 'completed' => true],
```

```php
        ['id' => 2, 'title' => 'Build a
microframework app', 'completed' => false],

        ['id' => 3, 'title' => 'Master
modern PHP', 'completed' => false],

    ];


    public function listTasks(Request
$request, Response $response): Response

    {

        $payload = json_encode($this-
>tasks);

        $response->getBody()-
>write($payload);

        return $response-
>withHeader('Content-Type',
'application/json');

    }


    public function getTask(Request
$request, Response $response, array $args):
Response

    {

        $taskId = (int) $args['id'];

        $task = null;
```

```php
        foreach ($this->tasks as $t) {

            if ($t['id'] === $taskId) {

                $task = $t;

                break;

            }

        }


        if ($task) {

            $payload = json_encode($task);

            $response->getBody()-
>write($payload);

            return $response-
>withHeader('Content-Type',
'application/json');

        }


        // Task not found, return a 404
response

        return $response->withStatus(404);

    }
```

```
    // ... We would continue to move the
logic for POST, PUT, and DELETE

    // into their own public methods here:
createTask, updateTask, deleteTask ...

}
```

We've created a class in the App\Controllers namespace and started moving our logic into its public methods. The method signatures are identical to the closures they are replacing. Now, we can update our public/index.php file to use this new controller. The process is straightforward: we remove the closure and replace it with an array containing the fully qualified class name as the first element and the method name as the second.

```php
<?php

// public/index.php


use App\Controllers\TaskController;

use Psr\Http\Message\ResponseInterface as
Response;

use Psr\Http\Message\ServerRequestInterface
as Request;

use Slim\Factory\AppFactory;


require __DIR__ . '/../vendor/autoload.php';
```

```php
$app = AppFactory::create();



// A simple "hello world" can remain a
closure.

$app->get('/', function (Request $request,
Response $response) {

    $response->getBody()->write("Welcome to
the Task API!");

    return $response;

});



// The routes for our resource now point to
controller methods.

$app->get('/tasks', [TaskController::class,
'listTasks']);

$app->get('/tasks/{id}',
[TaskController::class, 'getTask']);

// $app->post('/tasks',
[TaskController::class, 'createTask']);

// $app->put('/tasks/{id}',
[TaskController::class, 'updateTask']);

// $app->delete('/tasks/{id}',
[TaskController::class, 'deleteTask']);
```

```
$app->run();
```

Our `index.php` is already dramatically cleaner. It has returned
to its primary purpose: defining the application's routes and wiring
them to the code that handles them. The implementation details of
how those requests are handled are now neatly encapsulated within
the `TaskController`. This separation of concerns is a massive
step forward for maintainability.

Managing Dependencies with a DI Container

We've cleaned up our routing file, but we've introduced a new,
subtler problem. Our `TaskController` is currently responsible
for creating its own data—the `$tasks` array. In a real application,
a controller shouldn't contain data; it should *ask* for it from the
Model layer (e.g., a `TaskRepository` class that knows how to
talk to a database). The controller has a dependency. How do we
provide this dependency to it?

The wrong way would be to instantiate the `TaskRepository`
inside the controller's method. This is called a hard dependency,
and it makes our code rigid and difficult to test. We want to use
the Dependency Injection pattern we learned about in Chapter 4.
The controller should declare what it needs in its constructor, and
something else should be responsible for providing it.

Let's imagine we have a `TaskRepository` that provides our
data. Our controller would now look like this:

```php
<?php

// src/Controllers/TaskController.php


namespace App\Controllers;
```

```php
// Fictional TaskRepository for
demonstration

use App\Repositories\TaskRepository;

// ... other use statements ...


class TaskController

{

    // The controller now depends on a
repository.

    public function __construct(private
TaskRepository $repository)

        {

        }



    public function listTasks(Request
$request, Response $response): Response

        {

        // It asks the repository for the
data.

        $tasks = $this->repository-
>findAll();
```

```php
        $payload = json_encode($tasks);

        $response->getBody()-
>write($payload);

        return $response-
>withHeader('Content-Type',
'application/json');

    }



    // ... other methods would also use
$this->repository ...

}
```

This is a much better design. The controller is no longer concerned with where the tasks come from. But this creates a new question: if we're not instantiating the controller ourselves, who is creating it and passing in the `TaskRepository`? This is where a Dependency Injection (DI) container comes in.

A DI container (or service container) is a powerful object that acts as a central factory for all the important objects (or "services") in our application. You "teach" the container how to create various objects, and then you can simply ask it for an instance of a class when you need one. The container will automatically resolve and inject all of its dependencies for you. Slim is designed to integrate seamlessly with any DI container that follows the PSR-11 standard. A popular, lightweight, and powerful choice is PHP-DI. Let's add it to our project.

```
composer require php-di/php-di
```

Now, we can configure our application to use it. We'll create a new file to hold our container configuration, which keeps our index.php even cleaner.

```php
<?php

// bootstrap/container.php


use DI\ContainerBuilder;

use App\Repositories\TaskRepository; // Assuming this exists


// You would define interfaces and concrete implementations here

// For now, we'll just tell it how to make a TaskRepository

// which for this example, is just an object holding our array.


$containerBuilder = new ContainerBuilder();


$containerBuilder->addDefinitions([

    TaskRepository::class => function () {

        // In a real app, this would get a database connection
```

```php
        // and return a real repository
object.

        return new class {

            public function findAll(): array
{

                return [

                    ['id' => 1, 'title' =>
'Learn RESTful APIs', 'completed' => true],

                    ['id' => 2, 'title' =>
'Build a microframework app', 'completed' =>
false],

                ];

            }

            // ... findOne, save, delete
methods, etc. ...

        };

    },

]);


return $containerBuilder->build();
```

We've defined how to build a `TaskRepository`. Now we just need to tell Slim to use our new container. We do this by passing the container instance to `AppFactory::create()`.

```php
<?php

// public/index.php

use App\Controllers\TaskController;

use Slim\Factory\AppFactory;


require __DIR__ . '/../vendor/autoload.php';


// 1. Create the DI container from our
config file.

$container = require __DIR__ .
'/../bootstrap/container.php';


// 2. Pass the container into the
AppFactory.

AppFactory::setContainer($container);

$app = AppFactory::create();


// ... routes remain the same ...

$app->get('/tasks', [TaskController::class,
'listTasks']);

// ...
```

```
$app->run();
```

And now, everything just works. When a request for /tasks comes in, Slim sees that it needs to call a method on TaskController. It asks the DI container for an instance of TaskController. The container inspects TaskController's constructor, sees that it needs a TaskRepository, builds one according to our definition, and then uses it to construct the TaskController. Finally, Slim calls the listTasks method on the fully-formed controller object. This powerful, automatic "autowiring" of dependencies is a cornerstone of modern framework architecture.

The Onion Model: An Introduction to Middleware

Our application is now well-structured, but what about tasks that need to happen on *every* request, or on a large group of requests? For example, what if we want to log every API call? Or what if we need to check for an authentication token before allowing access to certain endpoints? We could add this logic to the beginning of every single controller method, but that would be a gross violation of the "Don't Repeat Yourself" (DRY) principle. This is the problem that middleware is designed to solve.

Middleware is a layer of code that sits between the web server and your controller. It can intercept an incoming request, do something with it, and then either pass it along to the next layer or decide to terminate the request early. It can also intercept the outgoing response on its way back to the client and modify it. The best way to visualize this is as an onion. The incoming request is the core, and it is wrapped in layers of middleware. To get to the core (your controller), the request must pass through each layer. After your controller creates a response, that response travels back out through the same layers in reverse order.

This pattern is incredibly powerful. A typical application might have middleware layers for:

- **Error Handling**: A top-level middleware that catches any exceptions thrown from deeper inside the application and converts them into a standardized JSON error response.

- **CORS**: Adds the necessary HTTP headers to allow cross-origin JavaScript requests.

- **Authentication**: Inspects the `Authorization` header and determines if the user is allowed to proceed.

- **Request Logging**: Records the URL, method, and status code of every request.

- **Body Parsing**: Decodes a JSON request body and makes it available as a simple array to the controller.

Crafting Our First Middleware

A middleware in the Slim ecosystem is any callable that matches a specific signature, but the cleanest way to write one is as a class that implements the PSR-15 `MiddlewareInterface`. This interface requires a single method: `process`. This method receives the current request object and a "request handler." The handler represents the next layer of the onion. The middleware's job is to eventually call `$handler->handle($request)` to pass control inward. The return value of that call is the response generated by the inner layers, which the middleware can then inspect or modify before returning it.

Let's create a very simple middleware that adds a custom header to every response, just to see the mechanism in action.

```php
<?php

//
src/Middleware/ExampleHeaderMiddleware.php
```

```php
namespace App\Middleware;


use Psr\Http\Message\ResponseInterface as
Response;

use Psr\Http\Message\ServerRequestInterface
as Request;

use Psr\Http\Server\MiddlewareInterface;

use Psr\Http\Server\RequestHandlerInterface
as RequestHandler;


class ExampleHeaderMiddleware implements
MiddlewareInterface

{

    public function process(Request
$request, RequestHandler $handler): Response

    {

        // First, pass the request to the
next layer to get a response.

        $response = $handler-
>handle($request);
```

```
        // Now, modify the response by
adding a header before returning it.

        return $response->withHeader('X-
Handled-By', 'Our-App');

    }

}
```

To enable this middleware for our entire application, we simply add it to the app object in our index.php file, before we define our routes.

```
<?php

// public/index.php

// ...

use App\Middleware\ExampleHeaderMiddleware;



// ...

$app = AppFactory::create();



// Add the middleware. Middleware is
executed in the reverse order it is added.

$app->add(new ExampleHeaderMiddleware());



// ... routes ...
```

```php
$app->run();
```

Now, if you run any request against your API, you will see the X-Handled-By: Our-App header in the response. Our onion now has its first layer.

Let's build a more practical example. A common task is parsing a JSON request body. Our controller methods for creating and updating tasks currently have to grab the raw body and call json_decode themselves. We can move this logic into a middleware that will do it for any POST, PUT, or PATCH request.

```php
<?php
//
src/Middleware/JsonBodyParserMiddleware.php


namespace App\Middleware;


// ... use statements ...


class JsonBodyParserMiddleware implements
MiddlewareInterface

{

    public function process(Request
$request, RequestHandler $handler): Response

    {
```

```php
        $contentType = $request-
>getHeaderLine('Content-Type');


        if (str_contains($contentType,
'application/json')) {

            $body = $request->getBody()-
>getContents();

            $data = json_decode($body,
true);


            if (json_last_error() ===
JSON_ERROR_NONE) {

                // It's valid JSON. Add it
to the request as a parsed attribute.

                $request = $request-
>withParsedBody($data);

            }

        }


        // Pass the (potentially modified)
request to the next layer.

        return $handler->handle($request);

    }

}
```

After adding this middleware to our app, our controller methods become much cleaner. They no longer need to deal with the raw request body at all. They can simply use the `getParsedBody()` method on the request object.

```php
<?php

// Inside TaskController.php


public function createTask(Request $request,
Response $response): Response

{

    // The middleware has already done the
heavy lifting!

    $newTaskData = $request-
>getParsedBody();


    // ... validation and creation logic ...

}
```

Grouping Routes and Selective Middleware

Applying a middleware to every single route isn't always what you want. An authentication middleware, for example, should protect the endpoints that modify data (POST, PUT, DELETE), but you might want to leave the endpoints for viewing data (GET) publicly accessible. Frameworks provide a way to group routes and apply middleware only to that specific group.

Slim's group() method allows you to define a common URL prefix and apply a set of middleware to all routes defined within it. This is the perfect tool for organizing our API endpoints and securing them. Let's imagine we have a very basic authentication middleware that just checks for a static API key in a header.

```php
<?php

// src/Middleware/ApiKeyAuthMiddleware.php


// A very basic, insecure example for
demonstration purposes only!

class ApiKeyAuthMiddleware implements
MiddlewareInterface

{

    public function process(Request
$request, RequestHandler $handler): Response

    {

        $apiKey = $request-
>getHeaderLine('X-Api-Key');



        if ($apiKey !== 'my-secret-key') {

            // Key is missing or invalid.
Terminate the request early.

            $response = new
\Slim\Psr7\Response();
```

```php
        $response->getBody()-
>write(json_encode(['error' =>
'Unauthorized']));

        return $response-
>withStatus(401)->withHeader('Content-Type',
'application/json');

    }



        // Key is valid. Pass to the next
layer.

        return $handler->handle($request);

    }

}
```

Now, in our index.php, we can restructure our routes to use this middleware selectively.

```php
<?php

// public/index.php

// ...



use App\Controllers\TaskController;

use App\Middleware\ApiKeyAuthMiddleware;
```

```php
// ... Add global middleware like body
parser, logger, etc.

// $app-
>add(JsonBodyParserMiddleware::class);



// Publicly accessible route

$app->get('/tasks', [TaskController::class,
'listTasks']);

$app->get('/tasks/{id}',
[TaskController::class, 'getTask']);



// Group routes that require authentication

$app->group('/tasks', function ($group) {

    $group->post('', [TaskController::class,
'createTask']);

    $group->put('/{id}',
[TaskController::class, 'updateTask']);

    $group->delete('/{id}',
[TaskController::class, 'deleteTask']);

})->add(new ApiKeyAuthMiddleware());



$app->run();
```

With this structure, a GET request to /tasks will work for anyone. However, a POST request to /tasks will first pass through our ApiKeyAuthMiddleware. If the X-Api-Key header is missing or incorrect, the middleware will immediately return a 401 Unauthorized response, and the TaskController::createTask method will never even be called. By combining routing, controllers, and middleware, we have created a clean, layered, and secure architecture that can serve as the foundation for a professional, production-ready web application.

CHAPTER NINE: Database Design and Interaction with PDO & ORMs

So far, our fledgling API has a rather serious flaw: it's completely forgetful. Every time our script finishes running—which is at the end of every single request—our array of tasks vanishes into the digital ether, only to be reborn with the same default data on the next request. To build a real application, we need persistence. We need a way to store our data in a safe, organized, and permanent home. That home is the database.

This chapter is where our application gets its long-term memory. We will begin by looking at the architectural blueprints for that memory: the fundamentals of relational database design. We'll learn how to structure our data logically before we write a single line of code to interact with it. Then, we will explore the two primary ways modern PHP applications talk to a database. First, we'll get our hands dirty with the direct, powerful, and built-in standard: PHP Data Objects, or PDO. Finally, we will ascend to a higher level of abstraction and explore the world of Object-Relational Mappers (ORMs), which allow us to interact with our database not as a series of tables and rows, but as the PHP objects we are already familiar with.

Designing Your Data's Home: Relational Database Fundamentals

Before we can store data, we must decide on its structure. For the vast majority of web applications, the tool of choice for this is the relational database management system (RDBMS), with popular examples being MySQL, MariaDB, and PostgreSQL. These systems organize data into tables, which are conceptually similar to spreadsheets. A table has columns, which define the attributes of the data (like name, email, price), and rows, where each row represents a single record or entity.

The "relational" part of the name is the secret sauce. It refers to the ability to define relationships between different tables. This is what allows us to model real-world connections, such as a customer having multiple orders, or a blog post having many comments. These relationships are established using keys.

A **primary key** is a column (or set of columns) that uniquely identifies each row in a table. The most common type of primary key is an auto-incrementing integer, often named `id`. No two rows in the same table can have the same primary key value.

A **foreign key** is a column in one table that refers to the primary key of another table. This is how we create a link. If a `tasks` table has a `user_id` column, that `user_id` is a foreign key that points to the `id` column in a `users` table. This simple mechanism allows us to model the fundamental relationships between our data.

There are three primary types of relationships:

1. **One-to-Many**: This is the most common relationship. One row in Table A can be linked to many rows in Table B, but one row in Table B can only be linked to one row in Table A. A classic example is a `User` having many `Tasks`. One user can have multiple tasks, but each task belongs to only one user. This is modeled with a foreign key (`user_id`) in the "many" table (`tasks`).

2. **One-to-One**: This is less common. One row in Table A is linked to exactly one row in Table B. For example, you might have a `users` table and a `user_profiles` table, where each user has only one profile. This is often used to split a very wide table into smaller, more logical parts.

3. **Many-to-Many**: This occurs when many rows in Table A can be linked to many rows in Table B. For instance, a `Post` can have many `Tags`, and a `Tag` can be applied to many `Posts`. This relationship cannot be modeled with a simple foreign key. It requires a third table, often called a

pivot or junction table. In our example, a `post_tag` table would be created with two columns: `post_id` and `tag_id`. Each row in this table represents a single link between a specific post and a specific tag.

Let's apply this to our API. We'll design a simple schema for our `users` and `tasks` tables.

Table: `users`

Column Name	Data Type	Notes
id	INT	Primary Key, Auto-Incrementing
name	VARCHAR(255)	The user's full name
email	VARCHAR(255)	The user's email address, must be unique
created_at	TIMESTAMP	Defaults to the current time when a row is created

Table: `tasks`

Column Name	Data Type	Notes
id	INT	Primary Key, Auto-Incrementing
user_id	INT	Foreign Key referencing `users.id`
title	VARCHAR(255)	The description of the task
completed	BOOLEAN	Defaults to `false`
created_at	TIMESTAMP	Defaults to the current time when a row is created

This simple, two-table schema establishes a one-to-many relationship: one user can have many tasks. A little bit of planning upfront goes a long way in preventing major headaches down the road. This practice of structuring tables to reduce data redundancy is known as normalization, a deep topic in its own right, but for now, this logical structure is all we need.

The Direct Approach: Talking to the Database with PDO

Now that we have a place to store our data, we need a way for our PHP code to communicate with it. The modern, built-in, and standard way to do this is with PDO, which stands for PHP Data Objects. PDO provides a consistent, object-oriented interface for accessing a wide variety of databases, from MySQL to PostgreSQL to SQLite. This is a huge advantage over the old, database-specific functions like `mysql_connect`, as it makes your data access code more portable.

The first step is establishing a connection. To do this, you instantiate the `PDO` class, providing it with a Data Source Name (DSN), a username, and a password. The DSN is a string that tells PDO which database driver to use and how to connect to the database.

```php
<?php


$host = '127.0.0.1';

$db   = 'my_app_db';

$user = 'db_user';

$pass = 'supersecretpassword';

$charset = 'utf8mb4';
```

```php
$dsn =
"mysql:host=$host;dbname=$db;charset=$charse
t";


$options = [

    PDO::ATTR_ERRMODE                  =>
PDO::ERRMODE_EXCEPTION,

    PDO::ATTR_DEFAULT_FETCH_MODE =>
PDO::FETCH_ASSOC,

    PDO::ATTR_EMULATE_PREPARES    => false,

];


try {

    $pdo = new PDO($dsn, $user, $pass,
$options);

} catch (\PDOException $e) {

    throw new \PDOException($e-
>getMessage(), (int)$e->getCode());

}
```

Let's break down the $options array, as this is crucial for
professional use. PDO::ATTR_ERRMODE =>
PDO::ERRMODE_EXCEPTION tells PDO to throw exceptions
when a database error occurs, which allows us to handle errors
cleanly with try...catch blocks.
PDO::ATTR_DEFAULT_FETCH_MODE =>

`PDO::FETCH_ASSOC` sets the default way PDO will return data rows as associative arrays, which is convenient. Finally, `PDO::ATTR_EMULATE_PREPARES => false` disables emulated prepared statements, forcing the use of true prepared statements, which is a key security feature.

This brings us to the single most important rule of database interaction: **you must always use prepared statements to pass user-supplied data into your SQL queries.** Failing to do so opens you up to a devastating vulnerability called SQL Injection.

Imagine you build a query by concatenating a variable directly into the string:

```
$sql = "SELECT * FROM users WHERE id = $userId"; // DANGER!
```

If a legitimate user provides an ID of `123`, the query works as expected. But what if a malicious user provides an ID of `123; DELETE FROM users`? Your final SQL string would become `SELECT * FROM users WHERE id = 123; DELETE FROM users`, and just like that, your entire user table is gone.

Prepared statements solve this problem by separating the SQL query itself from the data. The database compiles the query structure first and then safely inserts the data into the designated placeholders. The data is treated purely as data and can never be interpreted as part of the SQL command. The process involves three steps: prepare, bind, and execute.

```php
<?php


// 1. Prepare the SQL statement with placeholders

$sql = "SELECT id, name, email FROM users WHERE id = :id";
```

```php
$stmt = $pdo->prepare($sql);


// 2. Bind the value to the placeholder

$userId = 123;

$stmt->bindValue(':id', $userId,
PDO::PARAM_INT);


// 3. Execute the statement

$stmt->execute();


// 4. Fetch the result

$user = $stmt->fetch(); // Returns a single
row or false if not found
```

We used a named placeholder (:id), which makes the code very readable. You could also use positional placeholders (?), but named ones are generally preferred. For write operations like INSERT, UPDATE, or DELETE, the process is identical.

```php
<?php


$sql = "INSERT INTO tasks (user_id, title)
VALUES (:user_id, :title)";

$stmt = $pdo->prepare($sql);
```

```php
$stmt->execute([

    'user_id' => 123,

    'title' => 'My new task from PHP'

]);



// Get the ID of the row we just inserted

$newTaskId = $pdo->lastInsertId();



// For UPDATE or DELETE, you can check the
number of affected rows

$affectedRows = $stmt->rowCount();
```

Passing an associative array directly to execute() is a
convenient shortcut for binding multiple values. By consistently
using this prepare-bind-execute pattern, you effectively eliminate
the risk of SQL injection.

Bridging Two Worlds: The Object-Relational Mapper (ORM)

Working with PDO is powerful, direct, and secure. For many
applications, it's all you need. However, you may have noticed a
certain friction. Our application is built from objects
(TaskController, TaskRepository), but our database is
made of tables and rows. We spend a lot of time manually
translating back and forth: taking an object, pulling its data out to

bind to an `INSERT` statement, and then taking an associative array from a `SELECT` query and manually constructing an object from it. This conceptual gap between the object-oriented paradigm and the relational paradigm is known as the object-relational impedance mismatch.

An Object-Relational Mapper (ORM) is a library that is designed to solve this exact problem. It acts as an automated translator, bridging the gap between your database tables and your PHP classes. The core idea of an ORM is to map a database table to a PHP class (called an **Entity**). Each row in the table then corresponds to an instance of that class.

Instead of writing SQL, you interact with your objects. Want to save a new user? You create a `new User()` object, set its properties, and tell the ORM to save it. The ORM then generates and executes the necessary `INSERT` statement behind the scenes. Want to find a user? You ask the ORM for a user with a specific ID, and it returns a fully populated `User` object.

Using an ORM offers several compelling benefits:

- **Productivity:** You write significantly less boilerplate code. Complex `JOIN` queries can often be replaced by simple property access like `$user->getTasks()`.

- **Abstraction:** Your application code is decoupled from the specific SQL dialect of your database. In theory, switching from MySQL to PostgreSQL might only require changing a configuration setting.

- **Object-Oriented Approach:** It allows you to continue thinking in terms of objects throughout your entire application, which can lead to a cleaner, more cohesive design.

However, this abstraction is not without its costs:

- **Performance Overhead:** The translation layer adds a small amount of overhead compared to raw SQL.

- **Complexity:** Powerful ORMs can have a steep learning curve.

- **Leaky Abstraction:** For highly complex queries or performance-critical operations, you often still need to understand and sometimes even write raw SQL.

Choosing between PDO and an ORM is a trade-off between control and convenience. For simple applications or performance-critical paths, PDO is an excellent choice. For large, complex applications with a rich domain model, the productivity gains of an ORM are often indispensable.

An ORM in Action: A Taste of Doctrine

The two titans of the PHP ORM world are Eloquent (part of the Laravel framework) and Doctrine. Since our book focuses on components that can be used with any framework, we'll look at Doctrine, which is a powerful, standalone library used by Symfony and many other projects.

Let's see how we would define our `Task` entity using Doctrine. The modern way to configure the mapping between your object's properties and the table's columns is with PHP 8 attributes.

```php
<?php

// src/Entities/Task.php


declare(strict_types=1);


namespace App\Entities;
```

```php
use Doctrine\ORM\Mapping as ORM;


#[ORM\Entity]

#[ORM\Table(name: 'tasks')]

class Task

{

    #[ORM\Id]

    #[ORM\Column(type: 'integer')]

    #[ORM\GeneratedValue]

    private int $id;


    #[ORM\Column(type: 'string')]

    private string $title;


    #[ORM\Column(type: 'boolean')]

    private bool $completed = false;


    // We would also add properties and
mappings for user_id, created_at, etc.
```

```php
    // ... as well as getter and setter
methods for these private properties.


    public function getId(): int

    {

        return $this->id;

    }


    public function getTitle(): string

    {

        return $this->title;

    }


    public function setTitle(string $title):
void

    {

        $this->title = $title;

    }


    // ... other getters and setters
```

```
}
```

These attributes are metadata that tell Doctrine everything it needs to know. #[Entity] marks this as an entity class. #[Table] specifies the database table name. #[Column] maps a property to a column and defines its type. #[Id] and #[GeneratedValue] mark the primary key.

The central object in Doctrine is the **EntityManager**. It is the gateway through which you interact with the ORM. You use it to find, save, and delete entities.

Let's look at the basic CRUD operations with our Task entity.

```php
<?php



// Assume $entityManager has been configured
and instantiated elsewhere.



//  CREATING a new task

$task = new Task();

$task->setTitle('Learn Doctrine ORM');

$task->setCompleted(false);



// Tell the EntityManager to start managing
this new object.

$entityManager->persist($task);
```

```php
// Execute the INSERT query to save all
managed objects to the database.

$entityManager->flush();


echo "Created Task with ID: " . $task-
>getId() . "\n";


//   READING a task

$taskId = $task->getId();

$foundTask = $entityManager-
>find(Task::class, $taskId);


if ($foundTask !== null) {

    echo "Found Task: " . $foundTask-
>getTitle() . "\n";

}


//   UPDATING a task

if ($foundTask !== null) {

    $foundTask->setCompleted(true);
```

```
    // No need to call persist() on an
already managed object.

    $entityManager->flush(); // Executes the
UPDATE query.

    echo "Task updated.\n";

}



// DELETING a task

if ($foundTask !== null) {

    // Tell the EntityManager to remove this
object.

    $entityManager->remove($foundTask);

    $entityManager->flush(); // Executes the
DELETE query.

    echo "Task deleted.\n";

}
```

Notice the persist() and flush() methods. Doctrine uses a
pattern called "Unit of Work." When you persist() a new
object or change an existing one, Doctrine doesn't immediately run
a query. It keeps track of all the changes in memory. When you
call flush(), it calculates the most efficient set of queries
needed to synchronize all your changes with the database and
executes them in a single transaction.

Putting It All Together: Refactoring the Task Repository

Now we can circle back to our API and replace our in-memory data source with a real one. In Chapter 8, our `TaskController` depended on a `TaskRepository`. We can now create a concrete implementation of that repository using PDO. This demonstrates how, thanks to dependency injection, we can completely swap out the data layer without changing a single line of code in our controller.

First, let's define an interface for our repository. This contract ensures any implementation will have the methods our controller expects.

```php
<?php

//
src/Repositories/TaskRepositoryInterface.php

namespace App\Repositories;


interface TaskRepositoryInterface

{

    public function findAll(): array;

    public function findById(int $id):
?array;

}
```

Now, the PDO implementation:

```php
<?php

// src/Repositories/PdoTaskRepository.php
```

```php
namespace App\Repositories;


use PDO;


class PdoTaskRepository implements
TaskRepositoryInterface
{

    public function __construct(private PDO
$pdo)

    {

    }


    public function findAll(): array

    {

        $stmt = $this->pdo->query("SELECT *
FROM tasks");

        return $stmt->fetchAll();

    }


    public function findById(int $id):
?array

    {
```

```php
        $stmt = $this->pdo->prepare("SELECT
* FROM tasks WHERE id = :id");

        $stmt->execute(['id' => $id]);

        $task = $stmt->fetch();

        return $task ?: null;

    }



    // ... implementations for save(),
delete(), etc.

}
```

Finally, we update our DI container configuration to build and inject this new repository.

```php
<?php

// bootstrap/container.php

// ...



use App\Repositories\PdoTaskRepository;

use
App\Repositories\TaskRepositoryInterface;

use DI\ContainerBuilder;
```

```php
$containerBuilder->addDefinitions([

    // Instruction for how to create a PDO
connection object

    PDO::class => function () {

        $host = '127.0.0.1';

        $db   = 'my_app_db';

        $user = 'db_user';

        $pass = 'supersecretpassword';

        $dsn =
"mysql:host=$host;dbname=$db;charset=utf8mb4
";

        // ... options and return new
PDO(...)

    },



    // When something asks for the
interface, provide the concrete PDO
implementation

    TaskRepositoryInterface::class =>
\DI\autowire(PdoTaskRepository::class),

]);


return $containerBuilder->build();
```

Because our `TaskController`'s constructor asks for a `TaskRepositoryInterface`, the container knows to provide the `PdoTaskRepository`. And since `PdoTaskRepository` needs a `PDO` object, the container knows how to make that too, injecting it automatically. Our API is now powered by a real database, with a clean separation between the database access logic in our repository and the application logic in our controller.

CHAPTER TEN: User Authentication and Authorization

Our application now has a memory, a persistent database where it can store and retrieve data. This is a monumental step, but it immediately surfaces a new and critical question: whose data is it? In our current design, any anonymous person who can send a request to our API can create, view, update, and delete tasks. There is no concept of ownership, no privacy, and no security. This is the digital equivalent of a community bulletin board where anyone can post a note, but also cross out or tear down anyone else's note. To build a real, multi-user application, we must be able to answer two fundamental questions. The first is **Authentication**: "Who are you?" The second is **Authorization**: "What are you allowed to do?"

These two concepts, while closely related, are distinct and serve different purposes. Authentication is the process of verifying a user's claimed identity. It's the bouncer at the door checking your ID. When a user presents a username and password, the system checks if they match a known record to confirm they are who they say they are. Authorization, on the other hand, happens *after* successful authentication. It is the process of determining if an identified user has the necessary permissions to perform a specific action or access a particular resource. The bouncer authenticated you at the door, but authorization determines whether you have a VIP pass to enter the lounge upstairs. Getting this right is not just a feature; it is a foundational requirement for any application that handles user-specific data. It's the lock on the door, the key in the ignition, and the guardian of your users' trust.

Strategies for Verifying Identity

In the landscape of modern web applications, two primary strategies have emerged for managing user authentication: the traditional stateful approach using sessions, and the modern stateless approach using tokens. While both have their place, the stateless, token-based model has become the de facto standard for APIs, single-page applications (SPAs), and mobile clients, which is where our focus will be.

The classic approach is **Session-Based Authentication**. You've encountered this thousands of times. A user submits a login form. The server validates their credentials, creates a "session" on the server to store information about the logged-in user (like their user ID), and then sends a unique session identifier back to the user's browser, typically stored in an HTTP cookie. On every subsequent request, the browser automatically sends this cookie back. The server uses the identifier to look up the session data, confirm the user is logged in, and process the request. This model is stateful because the server must maintain the state of every user's session in memory or a database. While simple to grasp and effective for traditional server-rendered websites, it has drawbacks for modern APIs. It requires shared session storage to scale across multiple servers and doesn't work as elegantly with non-browser clients like mobile apps.

This brings us to the modern alternative: **Token-Based Authentication**. This approach is stateless. The server does not keep a record of who is logged in. Instead, after a user validates their credentials, the server generates a cryptographically signed, self-contained credential called a token. This token, which contains all the necessary information to identify the user, is sent back to the client. The client is then responsible for storing this token and sending it with every request to a protected resource, typically in the `Authorization` HTTP header. The server, upon receiving a request, can inspect the token, verify its digital signature to ensure it hasn't been tampered with, and identify the user, all without needing to look up anything in a session store. This stateless nature makes token-based systems incredibly scalable and flexible, which is why they are the perfect fit for the RESTful API we are building.

The dominant standard for these tokens is the **JSON Web Token**, or JWT (pronounced "jot"). A JWT is not an encrypted blob of data; it is a compact, URL-safe string that is simply encoded and signed. It consists of three parts, separated by dots: a Header, a Payload, and a Signature.

1. **Header**: This is a simple JSON object that typically identifies the signing algorithm being used (e.g., HMAC SHA-256 or RSA) and the type of the token, which is `JWT`. This JSON is then Base64Url encoded to form the first part of the JWT.

2. **Payload**: This is another JSON object that contains the "claims" of the token. Claims are statements about an entity (typically, the user) and some additional metadata. There are registered claims with recommended three-letter names, such as `sub` (Subject, the user's ID), `exp` (Expiration Time), and `iat` (Issued At). You can also add your own custom claims, like the user's role or name. Like the header, the payload is Base64Url encoded to form the second part of the JWT. It's crucial to remember this is just encoded, not encrypted. Anyone who intercepts the token can read its contents, so you must never put sensitive information in the payload.

3. **Signature**: This is the part that provides security. To create the signature, you take the encoded header, the encoded payload, a secret key that is known *only* to the server, and sign them with the algorithm specified in the header. The resulting signature ensures the token's integrity. If a malicious user tries to change the user ID in the payload, the signature will no longer be valid, and the server will reject the token.

The entire authentication flow is a clean, stateless dance. The client trades a long-term secret (a password) for a short-term, verifiable credential (the JWT), and then uses that credential to access the system for a limited time.

The Sacred Duty: Handling Passwords Securely

Before a user can log in, they must first register. This means our application will need to store their password, and how we do this is arguably the most critical security decision we will make. There is one rule that is absolute, inviolable, and non-negotiable: **You must never, ever, under any circumstances, store passwords in plaintext.** Storing a user's password directly is an act of gross negligence. If your database is ever compromised—and you must always assume it could be—every single one of your users' passwords would be exposed. Since many people reuse passwords across different services, a breach of your application could lead to their email, banking, and social media accounts being compromised as well.

The correct approach is to store a cryptographic **hash** of the password. A hash function is a one-way street. It takes an input (the password) and produces a fixed-size string of characters (the hash). This process is irreversible; you cannot get the original password back from its hash. It is also deterministic; the same password will always produce the same hash. When a user tries to log in, you don't compare their submitted password to the stored password. Instead, you hash the password they submitted and compare that hash to the hash you have stored in the database.

However, a simple hash is not enough. Malicious actors have pre-computed tables, called "rainbow tables," containing the hashes of billions of common passwords. If you use a simple hashing algorithm like MD5 or SHA-1, they can quickly look up the hash and find the original password. To defeat this, we must use a **salt**. A salt is a random string of data that is unique to each user. Before hashing the user's password, you append their unique salt to it. This means that even if two users have the same password, their stored hashes will be completely different because they have different salts. The salt is stored in the database alongside the password hash.

Fortunately, modern PHP makes this incredibly easy and secure. You do not need to generate salts or choose algorithms yourself. PHP provides a set of simple, powerful, built-in functions that handle everything: `password_hash()` and `password_verify()`. These functions are the only tools you should ever use for handling passwords in PHP.

The `password_hash()` function takes the plaintext password as input and an algorithm identifier. You should always use the `PASSWORD_DEFAULT` constant, which ensures your application will always use the latest and strongest hashing algorithm supported by PHP (currently, this is bcrypt). The function automatically generates a cryptographically secure salt, combines it with the password, hashes the result, and returns a single string that contains the algorithm, the salt, and the hash all bundled together.

```php
<?php

$plainTextPassword = 'MySecurePassword123';

$hashedPassword =
password_hash($plainTextPassword,
PASSWORD_DEFAULT);

// $hashedPassword is now something like
'$2y$10$7...long...random...string'

// This is what you store in your database's
`password` column.
```

When the user logs in, you use `password_verify()`. This function takes the plaintext password they just submitted and the full hash string from the database. It automatically extracts the salt and algorithm from the hash string, re-hashes the submitted password using that information, and performs a secure, timing-attack-safe comparison to see if the hashes match. It returns `true` if they do and `false` if they don't.

```php
<?php
```

```
$submittedPassword = $_POST['password']; //
The password from the login form

$hashFromDatabase = '...'; // The hash you
fetched for that user



if (password_verify($submittedPassword,
$hashFromDatabase)) {

    // Password is correct. Log the user in.

} else {

    // Password is incorrect.

}
```

By using these two functions, you are following current industry best practices for password security with almost no effort. There is no excuse for doing it any other way.

Implementing JWT Authentication in our API

Let's put this theory into practice. We'll add registration and login endpoints to our API and then create a middleware to protect our task-related endpoints. First, we need a library to handle the creation and verification of JWTs. A popular and well-maintained choice is firebase/php-jwt.

```
composer require firebase/php-jwt
```

We'll also need a users table in our database, as designed in the previous chapter, with id, name, email, and password columns. The password column should be a VARCHAR(255), as the output of password_hash() is a string of a fixed length (currently 60 characters, but it's good practice to allow for future algorithms).

Our first step is to create a registration endpoint. We'll need a new controller, AuthController, to handle this.

```php
<?php

// src/Controllers/AuthController.php

namespace App\Controllers;


use PDO;

use Psr\Http\Message\ResponseInterface as Response;

use Psr\Http\Message\ServerRequestInterface as Request;


class AuthController

{

    public function __construct(private PDO $pdo) {}


    public function register(Request $request, Response $response): Response

    {

        $data = $request->getParsedBody();
```

```php
$name = $data['name'] ?? '';

$email = $data['email'] ?? '';

$password = $data['password'] ?? '';


// Basic validation...

if (empty($name) || empty($email) ||
empty($password)) {

    // Return 400 Bad Request

}


// Hash the password

$hashedPassword =
password_hash($password, PASSWORD_DEFAULT);


$sql = "INSERT INTO users (name,
email, password) VALUES (:name, :email,
:password)";

$stmt = $this->pdo->prepare($sql);

$stmt->execute([

    'name' => $name,

    'email' => $email,
```

```php
        'password' => $hashedPassword

    ]);



    $response->getBody()-
>write(json_encode(['message' => 'User
registered successfully']));

    return $response->withStatus(201)-
>withHeader('Content-Type',
'application/json');

    }

}
```

Next, we create the login endpoint. This endpoint will verify the user's credentials and, if they are valid, issue a JWT.

```php
<?php

// Inside src/Controllers/AuthController.php



use Firebase\JWT\JWT;



class AuthController

{

    // ... __construct and register methods
...
```

```php
    public function login(Request $request,
Response $response): Response

    {

        $data = $request->getParsedBody();

        $email = $data['email'] ?? '';

        $password = $data['password'] ?? '';


        $stmt = $this->pdo->prepare("SELECT
* FROM users WHERE email = :email");

        $stmt->execute(['email' => $email]);

        $user = $stmt->fetch();


        if ($user &&
password_verify($password,
$user['password'])) {

            // Password is valid. Generate a
JWT.

            $secretKey = 'your-super-secret-
key-that-should-be-in-an-env-file';

            $issuedAt = time();

            $expire = $issuedAt + 3600; // 1
hour
```

```php
        $payload = [

            'iat' => $issuedAt,
// Issued at: time when the token was
generated

            'exp' => $expire,
// Expire

            'sub' => $user['id'],
// Subject (User ID)

        ];


        $token = JWT::encode($payload,
$secretKey, 'HS256');



        $response->getBody()-
>write(json_encode(['token' => $token]));

        return $response-
>withHeader('Content-Type',
'application/json');

    }


    // Invalid credentials

    $response->getBody()-
>write(json_encode(['error' => 'Invalid
credentials']));
```

```php
        return $response->withStatus(401)-
>withHeader('Content-Type',
'application/json');

    }

}
```

Now we need a middleware to protect our routes. This middleware will extract the token from the Authorization header, verify it, and if it's valid, attach the user's ID to the request for later use.

```php
<?php

// src/Middleware/JwtAuthMiddleware.php

namespace App\Middleware;


use Firebase\JWT\JWT;

use Firebase\JWT\Key;

use Psr\Http\Message\ResponseInterface as
Response;

use Psr\Http\Message\ServerRequestInterface
as Request;

use Psr\Http\Server\MiddlewareInterface;

use Psr\Http\Server\RequestHandlerInterface
as RequestHandler;

use Slim\Psr7\Response as SlimResponse;
```

```php
class JwtAuthMiddleware implements
MiddlewareInterface

{

    public function process(Request
$request, RequestHandler $handler): Response

    {

        $authHeader = $request-
>getHeaderLine('Authorization');

        if (empty($authHeader) ||
!preg_match('/Bearer\s+(.*)$/i',
$authHeader, $matches)) {

            return $this-
>createUnauthorizedResponse();

        }


        $token = $matches;

        $secretKey = 'your-super-secret-key-
that-should-be-in-an-env-file';


        try {

            $decoded = JWT::decode($token,
new Key($secretKey, 'HS256'));
```

```php
            // The token is valid. Add the
user ID to the request attributes.

            $request = $request-
>withAttribute('userId', $decoded->sub);

        } catch (\Exception $e) {

            // Token is invalid (expired,
bad signature, etc.)

            return $this-
>createUnauthorizedResponse();

        }


        return $handler->handle($request);

    }


    private function
createUnauthorizedResponse(): Response

    {

        $response = new SlimResponse();

        $response->getBody()-
>write(json_encode(['error' =>
'Unauthorized']));

        return $response->withStatus(401)-
>withHeader('Content-Type',
'application/json');
```

```
        }

}
```

Finally, we wire all this up in our routing file (`public/index.php`). We add the new routes for registration and login, and we apply our `JwtAuthMiddleware` to the routes that manage tasks.

```php
<?php

// public/index.php

// ...

use App\Controllers\AuthController;

use App\Controllers\TaskController;

use App\Middleware\JwtAuthMiddleware;


// ... container setup ...

$app = AppFactory::create();


// Public routes

$app->post('/register',
[AuthController::class, 'register']);

$app->post('/login', [AuthController::class,
'login']);
```

```php
// Protected routes

$app->group('/tasks', function ($group) {

    $group->get('', [TaskController::class,
'listTasks']);

    $group->get('/{id}',
[TaskController::class, 'getTask']);

    $group->post('', [TaskController::class,
'createTask']);

    $group->put('/{id}',
[TaskController::class, 'updateTask']);

    $group->delete('/{id}',
[TaskController::class, 'deleteTask']);

})->add(JwtAuthMiddleware::class); // DI
container will instantiate the middleware



$app->run();
```

With this in place, any attempt to access the /tasks endpoints without a valid JWT in the Authorization header will be rejected with a 401 Unauthorized error. Our API now has a secure front door.

Authorization: Now That You're In, What Can You Do?

Authentication gets a user through the door. Authorization dictates which rooms they are allowed to enter. Now that we know who the user is (thanks to our middleware adding the userId attribute to the request), we can enforce ownership rules. A user should be able to see and modify their own tasks, but not anyone else's. This is a critical step in building a secure, multi-tenant application.

The logic for this check belongs in the controller, right at the point where a specific resource is being accessed. Let's modify our `TaskController`'s `getTask` method to enforce this.

```php
<?php

// Inside src/Controllers/TaskController.php


public function getTask(Request $request,
Response $response, array $args): Response

{

    $taskId = (int) $args['id'];

    $currentUserId = $request-
>getAttribute('userId');



    $stmt = $this->pdo->prepare("SELECT *
FROM tasks WHERE id = :id");

    $stmt->execute(['id' => $taskId]);

    $task = $stmt->fetch();


    if (!$task) {

        return $response->withStatus(404);
// Not Found
```

```
    }


    // Authorization check

    if ($task['user_id'] !== $currentUserId)
{

        // The user is authenticated, but
not authorized to see this task.

        return $response->withStatus(403);
// Forbidden

    }



    $payload = json_encode($task);

    $response->getBody()->write($payload);

    return $response->withHeader('Content-
Type', 'application/json');

}
```

The key is the new authorization check. After we've confirmed the
task actually exists, we compare its user_id column with the ID
of the user making the request. If they don't match, we return a
403 Forbidden status code. This code is distinct from 401
Unauthorized. It tells the client, "I know who you are, and you
are a valid user, but you are specifically not allowed to access this
resource." This same logic must be applied to the updateTask
and deleteTask methods to ensure users can only modify their
own data.

For more complex applications, you might introduce **Role-Based Access Control (RBAC)**. This typically involves adding a `role` column to your `users` table (e.g., `'user'`, `'admin'`). Your authorization logic can then check this role. For example, a `DELETE /users/{id}` endpoint might be restricted to users with the `'admin'` role. As permission systems grow, this logic can be extracted into dedicated "Authorizer" or "Policy" classes to keep controllers clean and the rules centralized, but the fundamental principle remains the same: first authenticate the user, then authorize their action.

CHAPTER ELEVEN: Templating Engines and Frontend Integration

Up to this point, our application has been a ghost in the machine. It's a powerful, well-structured service that can manage users and tasks, secure its data, and talk to a database, but it communicates with the outside world exclusively through the cryptic language of JSON. For another computer program, a mobile app, or a JavaScript-powered frontend, this is the perfect dialect. For a human being using a web browser, however, it's about as welcoming as a screen full of binary. To build an application that people can actually see and interact with, we need to move beyond serving raw data and start serving finished documents. We need to generate HTML.

This chapter marks our transition from the backend's engine room to the frontend's presentation layer. We will bridge the gap between our PHP logic and the user's screen. While the modern web is replete with complex JavaScript frameworks that consume APIs to render interfaces, the traditional and still incredibly powerful approach is to generate the HTML directly on the server. This method, often called Server-Side Rendering (SSR), is fast, excellent for search engine optimization (SEO), and simpler for a vast range of applications. To do this professionally, however, we must avoid the pitfalls of the past. We will explore why directly mixing PHP logic and HTML is a recipe for disaster and how modern templating engines provide a clean, secure, and maintainable solution for building the "View" in our MVC architecture.

The temptation for a developer new to PHP, or one coming from an older style of coding, is to simply open a PHP file, type out some HTML, and then drop in PHP tags wherever data is needed. On the surface, this seems direct and intuitive. Why add another layer of abstraction when the language itself can be embedded directly into the document you want to create? This approach quickly reveals its flaws as soon as a project grows beyond a single page. Consider a simple script to display a list of tasks.

```
<!DOCTYPE html>

<html>

<head>

    <title>My Tasks</title>

</head>

<body>

    <h1>Tasks for <?php echo $username; ?></h1>

    <?php if (count($tasks) > 0): ?>

        <ul>

            <?php foreach ($tasks as $task): ?>

                <li style="<?php if ($task['completed']) { echo 'text-decoration: line-through;'; } ?>">

                    <?php echo $task['title']; ?>

                </li>

            <?php endforeach; ?>

        </ul>

    <?php else: ?>
```

```
    <p>You have no tasks!</p>

    <?php endif; ?>

</body>

</html>
```

This fragment of code, often called "spaghetti code," is a maintenance nightmare waiting to happen. The logic for presentation is inextricably tangled with the HTML structure. A web designer who knows nothing about PHP would be terrified to touch this file for fear of breaking the application. Even for the developer, it's difficult to read and reason about. More critically, it's dangerously insecure. The variables `$username` and `$task['title']` are being echoed directly into the HTML. If either of those variables contained malicious HTML or JavaScript submitted by a user, we would have just created a Cross-Site Scripting (XSS) vulnerability, one of the most common and damaging web security flaws. The browser would blindly execute the malicious script, potentially allowing an attacker to steal user data or hijack their session. We are manually responsible for escaping every single piece of data, a tedious task that is easy to forget.

This chaotic mixing of concerns violates the core principles of MVC. The View layer should be about presentation, not complex logic. A better way is needed, a tool that enforces separation, promotes security by default, and makes the process of building user interfaces a pleasure rather than a chore. This tool is the templating engine. A templating engine is a library that processes templates—text files containing a mix of static content and presentation-specific placeholders—and combines them with application data to produce a final output, usually HTML. It provides a simplified, sandboxed language specifically for presentation tasks, allowing you to keep your core application logic safely separate in your controllers and models.

In the PHP ecosystem, the most mature, powerful, and framework-agnostic templating engine is Twig. Originally created for the Symfony framework, Twig is now a standalone component used in thousands of projects, from custom applications to major platforms like Drupal. It solves all the problems of spaghetti code in one elegant package. It provides a clean, readable syntax that is easy for both developers and designers to learn. It enforces a strict separation between logic and presentation. Most importantly, it provides automatic, context-aware output escaping, making your application secure by default. When you use Twig, you are not just choosing a tool; you are adopting a professional philosophy for building the presentation layer of your application.

Getting started with Twig is a familiar process. We begin by adding it to our project using Composer. From your project's root directory, run the following command:

```
composer require twig/twig
```

Once installed, the core of Twig is its `Environment` class. This class acts as the central configuration and rendering object. When you instantiate it, you must tell it where to find your template files. This is done by providing it with a "loader." The most common loader is the `FilesystemLoader`, which you simply point to a directory where you will store all your templates. A common convention is to create a `templates/` directory at the root of your project for this purpose.

```php
<?php

// In a bootstrap file or at the start of
your application


require_once '/path/to/vendor/autoload.php';
```

```
// 1. Specify the directory where the
templates are stored

$loader = new
\Twig\Loader\FilesystemLoader('/path/to/temp
lates');



// 2. Instantiate the Twig environment

$twig = new \Twig\Environment($loader, [

    'cache' => '/path/to/tmp/cache', //
Optional: for performance in production

]);



// 3. Render a template

echo $twig->render('index.html', ['name' =>
'Fabien']);
```

The render() method is the workhorse of the library. Its first argument is the name of the template file to load, and the second is an associative array of data that you want to make available within that template. This array is the "context." The keys of the array become the variable names you can access inside the template. This simple, clean hand-off of data from your PHP logic to the template is the essence of how the system works.

The real beauty of Twig lies in its syntax, which is designed to be expressive, concise, and distinct from PHP itself. There are two primary types of delimiters: {{ ... }} is used to print the result of an expression or a variable to the output, and {% ... %} is used to execute a statement, like a loop or a conditional.

Let's rewrite our messy task list from earlier using a Twig template.

```twig
<!-- templates/tasks/list.html.twig -->

<!DOCTYPE html>

<html>

<head>

    <title>My Tasks</title>

</head>

<body>

    <h1>Tasks for {{ username }}</h1>


    {% if tasks is not empty %}

        <ul>

            {% for task in tasks %}

                <li class="{{ task.completed ? 'completed' : '' }}">

                    {{ task.title }}

                </li>

            {% endfor %}

        </ul>

    {% else %}
```

```
    <p>You have no tasks!</p>

    {% endif %}

</body>

</html>
```

The difference is immediate and profound. The code is cleaner and far more readable. The logic is limited to simple presentation concerns: checking if the `tasks` array is empty and looping over it. There are no distracting PHP tags. Most importantly, it is secure by default. The expressions `{{ username }}` and `{{ task.title }}` are automatically escaped by Twig. If the username variable contained `<script>alert('xss')</script>`, Twig would intelligently convert the angle brackets into their HTML entity equivalents (`&lt;` and `&gt;`), rendering the script harmlessly as plain text on the page. This single feature eliminates the most common vector for XSS attacks.

Twig's power extends far beyond simple variable substitution. It provides a rich set of tools to handle common presentation tasks. One of the most useful features is filters. A filter is a function that can be applied to a variable's output, invoked with a pipe symbol (`|`). They are chainable and provide a clean way to format data right where it's being displayed.

```
{# Capitalize a name #}

{{ user.name|capitalize }}



{# Format a date object #}

{{ post.published_at|date("F j, Y") }}
```

```
{# Truncate a long description #}

{{ product.description|slice(0, 150) ~ '...'
}}
```

```
{# Convert markdown to HTML (requires an
extension) #}

{{ comment.body|markdown_to_html }}
```

The tilde (~) is Twig's string concatenation operator. There are dozens of built-in filters for tasks like number formatting, URL encoding, and array manipulation, and it's straightforward to add your own custom filters, allowing you to encapsulate any presentation formatting logic into a reusable function.

While filters are great for transforming single pieces of data, the real key to building large, maintainable frontends is the ability to reuse entire sections of HTML. Twig provides two powerful mechanisms for this: includes and inheritance. The `include` statement is the simpler of the two. It allows you to pull the content of one template into another. This is perfect for small, reusable components like a site header, a footer, a navigation bar, or a sidebar. Instead of copying and pasting the same navigation HTML into every single page, you can define it once in a partial template and include it where needed.

```
<!-- templates/main.html.twig -->

<div class="page">

    <header>
```

```twig
    {% include
'partials/navigation.html.twig' %}

    </header>

    <main>

        <!-- Main page content goes here -->

    </main>

    <footer>

        {% include
'partials/footer.html.twig' %}

    </footer>

</div>



<!-- templates/partials/navigation.html.twig
-->

<nav>

    <a href="/">Home</a>

    <a href="/about">About</a>

    <a href="/contact">Contact</a>

</nav>
```

If include is like using a rubber stamp for small components, then template inheritance is like having a set of pre-printed stationery for your entire site. Inheritance is a powerful, "inside-out" way of thinking about your pages. You start by defining a single base layout template. This template contains the skeleton of your site's HTML, including the <html>, <head>, and <body> tags, links to your CSS and JavaScript files, and the common header and footer. Inside this skeleton, you define named, replaceable sections using the block tag.

```
<!-- templates/base.html.twig -->

<!DOCTYPE html>

<html>

<head>

    <meta charset="UTF-8">

    <title>{% block title %}My Awesome
Site{% endblock %}</title>

    <link rel="stylesheet"
href="/css/app.css">

</head>

<body>

    {% include
'partials/navigation.html.twig' %}


    <div class="content">

        {% block content %}{% endblock %}

    </div>
```

```twig
    {% include 'partials/footer.html.twig'
%}

</body>

</html>
```

This base template defines two editable areas: `title` and `content`. Now, an individual page template, like one for a blog post, doesn't need to contain all that boilerplate HTML. Instead, it can `extend` the base layout and simply provide the content for the defined blocks.

```twig
<!-- templates/blog/post.html.twig -->

{% extends 'base.html.twig' %}



{% block title %}{{ post.title }} | My
Awesome Site{% endblock %}



{% block content %}

    <h1>{{ post.title }}</h1>

    <div class="post-meta">

        Published on {{
post.published_at|date('M d, Y') }}

    </div>

    <div class="post-body">
```

```
    {{ post.body }}

  </div>

{% endblock %}
```

When Twig renders this `post.html.twig` template, it first loads the `base.html.twig` layout. It then "fills in the blanks," replacing the `title` and `content` blocks in the parent with the content defined in the child template. This pattern is the cornerstone of building complex yet consistent user interfaces. It ensures that every page on your site shares the same structure and assets, while allowing you to focus only on what is unique to each page.

To integrate this powerful tool into our Slim microframework application, we can leverage the DI container we set up in Chapter 8. Our goal is to make the Twig environment available as a service that our controllers can use. First, we'll create a factory in our container definition file that knows how to build the Twig object.

```php
<?php

// bootstrap/container.php

// ...

use Twig\Environment;

use Twig\Loader\FilesystemLoader;


// ...

$containerBuilder->addDefinitions([

    // ... other definitions like PDO ...
```

```php
    Environment::class => function () {

        $loader = new
FilesystemLoader(__DIR__ . '/../templates');

        return new Environment($loader, [

            // disable cache for development

            'cache' => false,

        ]);

    },

    // ...

]);
```

With this definition in place, our DI container now knows how to construct a Twig\Environment object. We can now create a controller that, instead of returning JSON, renders a user-facing web page. We can inject the Twig Environment directly into our controller's constructor.

```php
<?php

// src/Controllers/PageController.php

namespace App\Controllers;


use Psr\Http\Message\ResponseInterface as Response;
```

```php
use Psr\Http\Message\ServerRequestInterface
as Request;

use Twig\Environment;



class PageController

{

    public function __construct(private
Environment $twig)

    {

    }



    public function home(Request $request,
Response $response): Response

    {

        // Our controller's job is to fetch
data...

        $latestPosts = [ /* logic to get
posts from a repository */ ];

        $featuredProduct = [ /* logic to get
a product */ ];



        // ...and then pass that data to the
template for rendering.
```

```php
        $html = $this->twig-
>render('home.html.twig', [

            'posts' => $latestPosts,

            'product' => $featuredProduct

        ]);


        $response->getBody()->write($html);

        return $response;

    }

}
```

This controller perfectly demonstrates the separation of concerns. It is responsible for handling the request and orchestrating the retrieval of data from the Model layer. Once it has the data, its final job is to hand it off to the View layer (our Twig template) and write the resulting HTML into the response. The controller knows nothing about <h1> tags or CSS classes, and the template knows nothing about where the $posts variable came from. This clean division is the hallmark of a well-architected application.

It is important to understand where this server-side rendering approach fits into the modern web ecosystem. Our API from Chapter 7 was designed to serve data to a "client." That client is often a Single Page Application (SPA) built with a JavaScript framework like React or Vue. In that model, known as Client-Side Rendering (CSR), the server sends a nearly empty HTML file and a large JavaScript application. The JavaScript then makes API calls to fetch data and builds the user interface dynamically within the user's browser. CSR is excellent for highly interactive, application-like experiences, such as a project management dashboard or a real-time chat application.

Server-Side Rendering (SSR), the technique we've learned in this chapter, shines in different scenarios. For content-driven websites like blogs, news sites, and e-commerce platforms, SSR is often superior. The page arrives at the browser fully formed, making it faster for the user to see the content and significantly easier for search engines to crawl and index, which is critical for SEO. Many modern systems use a hybrid approach, where the server renders the initial page for speed and SEO, and then a JavaScript framework "hydrates" the page to take over and handle subsequent interactions. As a modern PHP developer, being proficient in both building data-centric APIs and rendering server-side views with a templating engine gives you the versatility to build the right backend for any type of frontend architecture.

CHAPTER TWELVE: Working with Forms and Validating User Input

Our application is taking shape. We have a robust backend capable of managing data, authenticating users, and even rendering user interfaces with a professional templating engine. Now we arrive at one of the most fundamental points of interaction in any web application: the form. Forms are the primary channel through which users communicate with our system. They are the gateways for registration, the control panels for updating profiles, the text boxes for leaving comments, and the buttons for purchasing products. Handling the data that flows through these gateways is a two-part process of immense importance. First, we must receive the data, and second, we must meticulously validate it. This second step is not merely a courtesy to the user; it is a non-negotiable cornerstone of security and data integrity. The golden rule of web development is simple and absolute: never, ever trust user input.

Before we can process data, we need a way for the user to send it. The venerable HTML `<form>` element has been the workhorse for this task since the dawn of the web. While its appearance can be styled in countless ways with CSS, its core mechanics are straightforward. A form is a container for input elements, and it is defined by two critical attributes: `action` and `method`. The `action` attribute specifies the URL where the form data should be sent when the user submits it. The `method` attribute defines the HTTP verb to be used for the request. For any action that creates, updates, or deletes data on the server, the method should always be `POST`. Using `GET` for such actions is a critical mistake, as it appends the form data to the URL, making it visible, easily bookmarked, and susceptible to being replayed accidentally. The `POST` method, by contrast, sends the data in the body of the HTTP request, which is the correct and secure approach for state-changing operations.

Inside the form, we have a variety of input elements to collect different kinds of data. The most common is the `<input>` tag, which can be configured with the `type` attribute to render as a text box (`type="text"`), a password field that obscures the characters (`type="password"`), an email field with basic client-side format checking (`type="email"`), a checkbox for on/off options (`type="checkbox"`), or a radio button for selecting one option from a group (`type="radio"`). For multi-line text, we use the `<textarea>` element, and for dropdown lists, the `<select>` element populated with `<option>` tags. Finally, a `<button type="submit">` or `<input type="submit">` gives the user a way to trigger the submission process, bundling up all the data in the form and sending it off to the URL specified in the `action` attribute.

Once the user clicks "submit," the browser sends a `POST` request to our server. In a traditional PHP script, this data would be available in the `$_POST` superglobal array. However, in our modern application built on PSR-7 standards, this raw interaction is abstracted away for better consistency and testability. Our Slim application's `Request` object provides a clean method, `getParsedBody()`, which we've already used. This method returns the POST data as an associative array, regardless of whether it was sent as a standard form submission or as JSON from an API client. This provides a unified way to access the incoming data within our controller methods. The crucial thing to remember is that at this stage, the data is completely raw and untrustworthy. It is a collection of strings that could contain anything from legitimate information to malicious code.

This is where validation begins its vital work. The reasons we validate are threefold. First and foremost is **security**. Without validation, an attacker could submit carefully crafted strings designed to exploit vulnerabilities in our application. They could inject malicious JavaScript to attack other users (Cross-Site Scripting) or manipulate our database queries (SQL Injection). Proper validation is our first and most important line of defense. The second reason is **data integrity**. Our database is designed with specific data types in mind: a `price` column expects a number, an `event_date` column expects a valid date, and a `status` column might expect one of a few specific string values. If we allow malformed data into our database, we corrupt our application's state, leading to bugs and unpredictable behavior. The third reason is **user experience (UX)**. When a user makes a mistake—forgets a required field or types an invalid email address—our application should provide clear, immediate, and helpful feedback so they can correct it easily.

It is essential to distinguish between client-side and server-side validation. Client-side validation happens in the user's browser before the form is even submitted. This is achieved using HTML5 attributes like `required`, `minlength`, `maxlength`, and `pattern`, or with custom JavaScript logic. This type of validation is a fantastic UX enhancement because it provides instant feedback. However, it must be treated as a convenience, not a security measure. Any user with basic browser developer tools can easily disable JavaScript or remove the HTML attributes and submit any data they wish. Therefore, **server-side validation is the only validation that matters for security and data integrity.** It is the final, authoritative check that must be performed on every piece of incoming data, every single time.

To truly understand the process, let's build a validation routine manually. Imagine a registration form with fields for a username, email, and password. Our controller action that receives this POST request would perform a series of checks and collect any failures in an `$errors` array. This array acts as a report card for the submission. If, at the end of all the checks, the `$errors` array is empty, we know the data is safe to process. If it contains any messages, we know the submission was invalid. In that case, we must not simply show an error page. The correct user experience is to re-render the original form, but this time, we pass the `$errors` array and the user's original submitted data back to the template.

```php
<?php
```

```php
// Inside a controller method

$data = $request->getParsedBody();

$errors = [];


if (empty($data['username'])) {

    $errors['username'] = 'Username is
required.';

}


if (!filter_var($data['email'],
FILTER_VALIDATE_EMAIL)) {

    $errors['email'] = 'A valid email
address is required.';

}


if (strlen($data['password']) < 8) {

    $errors['password'] = 'Password must be
at least 8 characters long.';

}


if (!empty($errors)) {
```

```php
    // Validation failed. Re-render the form
with errors and old input.

    return $this->twig->render($response,
'register.html.twig', [

        'errors' => $errors,

        'old' => $data

    ]);

}
```

```php
// Validation passed! Proceed with creating
the user...
```

Passing the old data back is crucial. It allows us to repopulate the form fields so the user doesn't have to re-type everything they had already entered correctly. In our Twig template, we can then conditionally display the errors and set the values of the input fields.

```twig
<!-- In register.html.twig -->

<form method="POST" action="/register">

    <div>

        <label
for="username">Username</label>

        <input type="text" name="username"
value="{{ old.username ?? '' }}">

        {% if errors.username %}
```

```
    <span class="error">{{
errors.username }}</span>

    {% endif %}

</div>

<!-- ... other fields similarly ... -->
</form>
```

This manual approach works and clearly illustrates the fundamental flow of validation: check, collect errors, and re-render on failure. However, for a form with ten or twenty fields, writing this much boilerplate if/else logic becomes incredibly tedious and error-prone. This is a solved problem, and the professional solution is to use a dedicated validation library.

Libraries like respect/validation or rakit/validation provide a fluent, expressive, and powerful Domain-Specific Language (DSL) for defining validation rules. They abstract away the repetitive conditional logic, allowing you to clearly declare the "contract" that your input data must adhere to. Let's refactor our validation logic using respect/validation. After installing it with composer require respect/validation, we can replace our manual checks with a much more declarative and readable chain of rules.

```php
<?php

use Respect\Validation\Validator as v;

use Respect\Validation\Exceptions\NestedValidationException;
```

```php
// Inside a controller method

$data = $request->getParsedBody();

$errors = [];



$validator = v::key('username',
v::stringType()->length(3, 25), 'Username is
required and must be between 3 and 25
characters.')

                ->key('email', v::email(),
'Please provide a valid email address.')

                ->key('password',
v::stringType()->length(8, null), 'Password
must be at least 8 characters.');


try {

    $validator->assert($data);

    // Validation passed!

} catch (NestedValidationException $e) {

    // Validation failed.

    $errors = $e->getMessages();

}
```

```
if (!empty($errors)) {

    // Re-render the form...

}

// Proceed...
```

This approach is vastly superior. The rules are clear, self-documenting, and chained together logically. The library provides hundreds of pre-built rules for everything from checking credit card numbers to validating IP addresses, saving you from having to write complex regular expressions or logic. It handles the collection of error messages for you, providing a clean and consistent way to manage the validation process. Using a dedicated library is the standard for professional PHP development.

Now, let's place this entire process into the larger context of our MVC application. A typical form submission workflow involves two distinct controller actions mapped to two different routes. The first action handles the GET request to display the form. Its only job is to render the blank template. The second action handles the POST request that is generated when the user submits the form. This is where the validation logic lives. This separation keeps our controllers clean and adheres to the principle of a method having a single responsibility.

The POST action follows a clear sequence of steps: receive data, validate data. If validation fails, it re-renders the form with the errors and old input. If validation succeeds, it performs the necessary business logic, such as saving a new user to the database. After a successful operation, it should not simply render a "success" template. Doing so would leave the user's browser on the POST URL. If they were to hit refresh, the browser would prompt them to resubmit the form data, potentially creating a duplicate record. To prevent this, we use a crucial pattern known as **Post/Redirect/Get (PRG)**. After the POST request is successfully processed, the server responds not with HTML, but with a `302 Found` redirect header, pointing the browser to a different URL (like a login page or a "registration successful" page). The browser then makes a brand new `GET` request to this new URL. This clears the `POST` data from the browser's history, making a refresh safe.

One final, critical piece of the form security puzzle is defending against Cross-Site Request Forgery (CSRF). A CSRF attack occurs when a malicious website tricks an authenticated user's browser into making an unwanted request to your application. For example, a user might visit a malicious site that contains a hidden form that automatically submits a `POST` request to `/my-app/delete-account`. Because the user's browser automatically includes their session cookie with the request, your application would see a valid, authenticated request to delete the account and would dutifully comply, all without the user's knowledge or consent.

The standard defense is the Synchronizer Token Pattern. The process is simple: when your server renders a form, it generates a unique, single-use, unpredictable string called a CSRF token. It embeds this token in a hidden input field within the form and also stores a copy in the user's session. When the form is submitted, the server checks if the token from the submitted form data matches the one in the session. If they match, the request is legitimate. If they don't match or the token is missing, the request is rejected. An attacker on another website has no way of knowing what the correct token is for the user's session, so their forged request will fail. Implementing this manually is possible, but it's a perfect job for middleware. Libraries like `slim/csrf` provide middleware that handles this entire process automatically. You simply add the middleware to your application, and then use a function it provides to inject the hidden input field into your forms. The middleware intercepts all incoming `POST` requests, performs the token check, and protects your entire application.

Finally, a brief word on a special type of user input: file uploads. Handling files requires a few extra steps. The HTML form must have the `enctype="multipart/form-data"` attribute. In our PSR-7 application, uploaded file information is not in the old `$_FILES` superglobal but is accessed via `$request->getUploadedFiles()`. This method returns an array of uploaded file objects, which provide methods to get the original filename, size, MIME type, and, most importantly, to move the uploaded temporary file to a permanent location. File uploads are a major security risk. You must validate the file type (using server-side tools like `finfo_file`, not just the client-provided information), enforce a strict file size limit, generate a new, safe filename to prevent directory traversal attacks, and ideally, store the files in a directory that is not directly accessible from the web. By combining robust validation, the PRG pattern, and CSRF protection, we can build forms that are not only user-friendly but also secure fortresses for our application's data.

CHAPTER THIRTEEN: Asynchronous PHP: Promises and Event Loops

For twelve chapters, we have operated within a comfortable and familiar paradigm, one that has defined PHP since its inception. It is the world of the synchronous request-response cycle. A user's browser sends a request, our web server hands it to a PHP process, and that process executes our script from top to bottom, one line at a time. If our script needs to query a database, it sends the query and then patiently waits, doing absolutely nothing, until the database responds. If it needs to call a third-party API, it makes the call and again, it waits. Only when the final line of the script has been executed is the complete response sent back to the user. This model is simple, predictable, and has powered a vast portion of the web for decades. It is also, for a certain class of problems, remarkably inefficient.

The bottleneck in most web applications is not the speed of the CPU; it is the time spent waiting for Input/Output, or I/O. Waiting for the network, waiting for the disk, waiting for the database—these are the moments where our powerful server processors sit idle, twiddling their digital thumbs. In the synchronous world, a single PHP process is tied up for the entire duration of this waiting period, unable to do any other useful work. If you have a hundred users all making slow API calls at once, you need a hundred PHP processes to handle them, consuming a significant amount of memory. This is the problem that asynchronous programming is designed to solve. It represents a fundamental shift in thinking: instead of waiting for a slow operation to finish, we can start the operation, move on to other tasks, and be notified later when the result is ready. This non-blocking approach allows a single PHP process to juggle thousands of concurrent I/O-bound tasks, dramatically increasing throughput and efficiency for the right kind of workload.

At the very heart of any asynchronous system is a concept known as the event loop. The event loop is the engine that makes non-

198

blocking I/O possible. Imagine a chef in a kitchen. The synchronous chef takes an order, walks to the stove, puts a pot of water on, and stands there watching it until it boils. Only then do they start chopping vegetables for the same dish. The asynchronous chef, by contrast, puts the pot on the stove and then immediately turns to chop vegetables. They know they don't need to watch the pot; it will whistle when it's ready. The event loop is that ability to "do something else" while waiting. It is a single-threaded, continuously running loop that maintains a list of tasks. Its job is simple: check for any I/O operations that have completed (e.g., data has arrived on a network socket, a timer has expired) and then execute the corresponding callback function that was registered for that event.

In the PHP world, the event loop isn't a built-in language feature. It's provided by powerful open-source libraries that have brought this new paradigm to the language. The two most prominent pure-PHP implementations are ReactPHP and Amp. Both provide robust, battle-tested event loop implementations that allow you to write high-concurrency applications without leaving the comfort of the PHP ecosystem. A third, incredibly powerful player is Swoole, which is not a library but a PHP extension written in C. By moving the event loop and network management to a lower level, Swoole offers a significant performance boost, effectively turning PHP into a first-class citizen for building high-performance network services, comparable to platforms like Node.js or Go. While their implementations differ, the core concept of a central loop dispatching events is the foundation they all share.

The most immediate challenge in an event-driven world is managing the flow of your program. If you simply register a callback function for every asynchronous operation, your code can quickly devolve into a deeply nested, unreadable tangle known as "callback hell." This is a problem that early Node.js developers encountered with painful frequency. To solve this, asynchronous PHP libraries adopted a powerful abstraction to represent a future result: the Promise. A Promise is a placeholder object. It is a stand-in for a value that is not yet known because the asynchronous operation that will produce it has not yet completed. It is a "promise" that you will eventually get a value, or an error.

A Promise can be in one of three states. When first created, it is in the **pending** state. It is waiting for the underlying operation to finish. If the operation completes successfully, the promise transitions to the **fulfilled** (or resolved) state, and it now holds the resulting value. If the operation fails for any reason, the promise transitions to the **rejected** state, holding the error or exception that caused the failure. The key to using promises is the .then() method. This method allows you to register callbacks that will be executed when the promise is eventually fulfilled or rejected. This enables you to chain asynchronous operations together in a way that is clean, linear, and far more readable than nested callbacks.

```php
<?php

// A simplified example using a promise-
based library



$promise =
someAsyncFunctionThatReturnsAPromise();



$promise->then(

    // This function runs on success
(fulfillment)

    function ($value) {

        echo "Operation succeeded with
value: " . $value;

    },
```

```php
    // This function runs on failure
(rejection)

    function (\Exception $error) {

        echo "Operation failed with error: "
. $error->getMessage();

    }

);


echo "This line will execute immediately,
before the promise resolves.";
```

By chaining `.then()` calls, you can create a clear sequence of asynchronous steps. The output of one step is automatically passed as the input to the next, and an error at any point in the chain will skip the remaining success callbacks and bubble down to the nearest error handler, much like a `try...catch` block. This structured approach to handling asynchronous results is what makes the paradigm manageable.

While promises are a massive improvement over raw callbacks, the syntax still feels inherently different from the synchronous code we are used to. The latest evolution in asynchronous programming, which has made its way into PHP via libraries like Amp and Swoole, and is now powered by a core language feature called Fibers (introduced in PHP 8.1), is the concept of coroutines. Coroutines, often used with `async/await` syntax in other languages, allow you to write asynchronous, non-blocking code that looks and feels almost identical to synchronous, blocking code. A coroutine is a function that can have its execution paused and resumed. When a coroutine encounters an I/O operation (like an API call), instead of blocking the entire process, it "yields" control back to the event loop. The event loop can then run other tasks. When the I/O operation completes, the event loop automatically resumes the coroutine right where it left off, with the result of the operation now available.

```php
<?php

// A conceptual example using Amp's
coroutine/fiber support



Amp\async(function () {

    // This code looks synchronous, but it
is not blocking the event loop.

    echo "Fetching user data...\n";



    // The `await` keyword pauses this
function, allowing the event loop

    // to work on other things until the
HTTP call is complete.

    $response =
Amp\Http\Client\request('https://api.example
.com/user/1');

    $userData = $response->getBody()-
>buffer();



    echo "User data received. Fetching
user's posts...\n";
```

```
    // This second call also happens
asynchronously.

    $response =
Amp\Http\Client\request('https://api.example
.com/user/1/posts');

    $postsData = $response->getBody()-
>buffer();


    echo "All data fetched.
Processing...\n";

});
```

This is the holy grail of asynchronous programming: the performance benefits of non-blocking I/O combined with the readability and straightforward logic of synchronous code. The complexity of promises and callbacks is abstracted away by the runtime, allowing you to focus on your application's logic. This ergonomic improvement, powered by Fibers, is what makes modern asynchronous PHP a truly viable and compelling option.

So, where does this new capability actually fit? It's important to recognize that asynchronous PHP is not a silver bullet. For a typical content-heavy website like a blog or a brochure site running on a standard PHP-FPM and Nginx stack, the traditional synchronous model is often perfectly adequate and simpler to manage. Asynchronous PHP shines in applications that are heavily I/O-bound and require high concurrency. One of the prime use cases is building **high-concurrency API servers**. Imagine an API that serves a popular mobile application. You might have thousands of users connected simultaneously over slow, unreliable mobile networks. In a synchronous model, each of those connections would tie up a PHP-FPM process, consuming a large amount of server memory. An asynchronous server built with Amp, ReactPHP, or Swoole can handle thousands of these concurrent connections within a single PHP process, using a fraction of the memory, because it doesn't waste resources waiting for slow clients.

Another powerful use case is performing **concurrent I/O tasks**. Consider a page in your application that needs to display data aggregated from three different internal microservices. In the synchronous world, you would have to make these API calls one after the other: call Service A, wait for the response, call Service B, wait, call Service C, wait. If each service takes 200 milliseconds to respond, the total time spent waiting is 600ms. With an asynchronous approach, you can initiate all three API calls at the same time. The event loop will manage all three network connections concurrently. The total wait time is now only as long as the slowest of the three calls, likely just over 200ms. You can use promise combinators like `Promise\all()` to wait for a collection of promises to be fulfilled and then process their results together. This can lead to dramatic performance improvements for complex, distributed systems.

Finally, asynchronous PHP is the natural foundation for building **real-time applications**. Services like chat servers, live notification systems, streaming data dashboards, and interactive multi-user games all require the server to maintain a large number of long-lived, persistent connections. The traditional request-response model is completely unsuited for this, as a PHP script normally dies at the end of each request. An asynchronous server, by contrast, is a long-running process. It can accept a connection and keep it open indefinitely, allowing for two-way communication between the server and the client. This is the domain of WebSockets, a technology that provides this persistent connection over a single TCP socket, and it is a topic we will explore in detail in the very next chapter. Asynchronous PHP provides the underlying engine that makes handling thousands of these WebSocket connections feasible.

Let's ground this theory in a practical example. We'll build a simple command-line script using ReactPHP that concurrently checks the status of several websites. This script will demonstrate the power of initiating multiple I/O-bound tasks at once. First, we need to install the necessary components: an event loop, an HTTP client, and promise utilities.

```
composer require react/event-loop react/http
react/promise
```

Now we can write our script. The goal is to make HTTP requests to a list of URLs simultaneously and report on their status codes as the responses come in.

```php
<?php

// check_sites.php

require 'vendor/autoload.php';



use React\Http\Browser;

use React\Promise\PromiseInterface;



// 1. We start by getting an instance of the
event loop.

$loop = React\EventLoop\Loop::get();

// 2. We create a promise-based HTTP client
(Browser).

$browser = new Browser($loop);
```

```php
$urls = [

    'https://www.google.com',

    'https://www.github.com',

    'https://www.php.net',

    'https://thissitedoesnotexist.invalid',

];


foreach ($urls as $url) {

    echo "Checking $url...\n";


    // 3. For each URL, we initiate a GET
request. This is non-blocking.

    // The `then()` method registers our
callbacks.

    $promise = $browser->get($url);

    $promise->then(

        function
(Psr\Http\Message\ResponseInterface
$response) use ($url) {

            // Success callback

            echo "$url returned status code:
" . $response->getStatusCode() . "\n";
```

```php
            },

        function (Exception $error) use
($url) {

            // Error callback

            echo "Failed to fetch $url: " .
$error->getMessage() . "\n";

        }

    );

}



// 4. This is the crucial step. We start the
event loop. The script will

// now pause here and only exit once all
pending I/O operations are complete.

$loop->run();



echo "All checks complete.\n";
```

When you execute this script with php check_sites.php, you will notice something interesting. You won't see the output appear sequentially, waiting for each site to respond. Instead, the "Checking..." messages will all appear almost instantly. Then, as the DNS lookups and HTTP requests for each site complete, their status messages will appear in whatever order they happen to finish. The fast ones will report back first, and the request to the invalid domain will eventually time out and trigger its error callback. We have successfully performed four network operations concurrently, a feat that would be clumsy and inefficient to replicate in a purely synchronous model.

It's important to understand the different deployment and execution models. Libraries like ReactPHP and Amp are typically used to build applications that run as long-lived processes, often started from the command line. This is a departure from the traditional PHP-FPM model where a master process manages a pool of short-lived worker scripts. When you build an HTTP server with these libraries, you are creating a single PHP script that *is* the web server. It binds directly to a network port and runs continuously, handling requests as they arrive on its event loop.

Swoole takes this a step further. As a C extension, it provides a highly optimized, multi-process event-driven server that you configure and run. It offers features like a built-in coroutine scheduler, memory sharing between processes, and native support for WebSockets, all with performance that often surpasses its pure-PHP counterparts. The trade-off is the added complexity of installing and managing a PECL extension and learning its specific APIs and deployment model. The choice between a pure-PHP solution and an extension like Swoole often comes down to a balance between ease of use, portability, and the raw performance requirements of your project.

Asynchronous programming in PHP is no longer a niche, experimental concept. It is a mature, powerful, and increasingly mainstream paradigm for building a specific class of high-performance, I/O-bound applications. While it requires a shift in thinking away from the familiar synchronous flow, the payoff in terms of efficiency and capability can be enormous. By understanding the roles of the event loop, promises, and coroutines, you have unlocked a new toolkit that enables you to tackle challenges that were once considered outside the realm of PHP's capabilities, pushing the boundaries of what you can build with the language.

CHAPTER FOURTEEN: Building Real-time Applications with WebSockets

For most of its history, the web has communicated through a polite but rigid dialogue. The client, a web browser, speaks first by making an HTTP request. The server then listens, formulates a response, and speaks back. After its reply, the server falls silent, waiting patiently for the client to initiate the next conversation. This request-response cycle is the bedrock of the web, a simple and scalable model that has served us incredibly well for displaying documents and submitting forms. For an entire class of modern, interactive applications, however, this turn-based conversation is frustratingly inadequate. What if the server has something new to say, but the client hasn't asked a question yet?

This is the central challenge of real-time communication. How do you build a chat application where messages appear instantly without the user having to hit a refresh button? How do you create a live stock ticker, a collaborative document editor, or a dashboard that updates with breaking news? Early attempts to solve this problem were clever workarounds built on the limitations of HTTP. **Polling** involved the client repeatedly asking the server, "Anything new?" every few seconds, a process that was inefficient and generated a huge amount of unnecessary network traffic. A refinement, **long-polling**, had the client make a request that the server would hold open, only responding when it actually had new information, which was better but still carried the overhead of repeatedly establishing new HTTP connections.

These solutions felt like trying to have a fluid conversation using only postcards. The true breakthrough arrived with the standardization of WebSockets. A WebSocket is not a workaround; it is a fundamental enhancement to the web's communication protocol. It provides a mechanism to upgrade a standard HTTP connection into a persistent, bidirectional, full-duplex communication channel. In simple terms, after a brief, one-time handshake, both the client and the server can send messages to each other at any time, for as long as the connection is open. The turn-based dialogue becomes a live phone call. This capability is the engine behind the modern real-time web, and thanks to the power of the asynchronous tools we explored in the previous chapter, it is a capability that modern PHP is fully equipped to command.

The journey to a WebSocket connection begins, perhaps surprisingly, with a standard HTTP request. The client cannot simply open a raw TCP socket to the server, as firewalls and other network intermediaries are configured to expect and handle HTTP traffic on ports 80 and 443. The WebSocket protocol was cleverly designed to piggyback on this existing infrastructure. The process, known as the WebSocket handshake, is an "upgrade" request. The client sends a normal HTTP GET request to the server, but it includes a special set of headers that signal its intent.

These headers are a formal invitation to switch from the HTTP protocol to the WebSocket protocol. The `Upgrade: websocket` header is the explicit declaration of this desire. The `Connection: Upgrade` header informs any intermediary proxies that the connection is about to change protocols. The `Sec-WebSocket-Version` header specifies which version of the protocol the client wishes to use (typically 13). The most interesting header is `Sec-WebSocket-Key`. This contains a randomly generated, Base64-encoded string. It does not provide any security; rather, it serves as a challenge to the server to prove that it actually understands the WebSocket protocol and isn't just a simple HTTP server that might misinterpret the subsequent data stream.

A WebSocket-aware server, upon receiving this request, performs a specific calculation. It takes the value from the `Sec-WebSocket-Key`, appends a globally defined unique string ("258EAFA5-E914-47DA-95CA-C5AB0DC85B11", often called the "magic string"), calculates the SHA-1 hash of the combined string, and then Base64-encodes the resulting hash. This final value is sent back in the `Sec-WebSocket-Accept` response header. When the client receives the response, it performs the same calculation and verifies that the server's result matches. This confirmation prevents a naive server or a caching proxy from accidentally establishing a broken WebSocket connection. If this check passes and the server is willing to upgrade, it responds with the special HTTP status code `101 Switching Protocols`. At this moment, the conversation ceases to be HTTP. The underlying TCP connection is handed over to the WebSocket protocol, and the real-time, bidirectional communication can begin.

It is critical to understand that this kind of persistent connection management is fundamentally incompatible with the traditional PHP-FPM execution model. A standard PHP-FPM worker is designed to handle a single request and then die, cleaning up all its resources. It cannot hold a connection open indefinitely. This is precisely why the asynchronous, event-driven architecture from the previous chapter is not just an option, but a prerequisite. To build a WebSocket server in PHP, we need a long-running script powered by an event loop, capable of holding thousands of connections open simultaneously and reacting to incoming data as it arrives.

Fortunately, we don't need to implement the complex WebSocket protocol from scratch. The PHP community has produced excellent libraries for this purpose, and one of the most established and well-designed is Ratchet. Ratchet is a WebSocket library for PHP that is built on top of the components from the ReactPHP ecosystem. It provides a clean, event-driven architecture that makes building real-time applications remarkably straightforward. The first step is to add it to our project using Composer.

```
composer require cboden/ratchet
```

Ratchet's architecture is a beautiful example of layered, single-responsibility components. To create a server, you typically stack three objects. At the lowest level is the `React\Socket\Server`, which handles the raw TCP connections. This is wrapped by Ratchet's `IoServer`, which manages the client connections and the event loop. This is then wrapped by an `HttpServer`, which understands the HTTP protocol and is responsible for handling the initial upgrade handshake. Finally, this is wrapped by a `WsServer` (WebSocket Server), which handles the WebSocket-specific protocol details, like decoding data frames. The innermost component is your application itself—a class that you write to define how the server should actually behave when it receives messages.

This application class must implement Ratchet's `MessageComponentInterface`. This interface is the heart of your server-side logic and requires you to define four methods, each corresponding to a key event in a connection's lifecycle: `onOpen()`, `onMessage()`, `onClose()`, and `onError()`. These events are triggered by the server when a client connects, sends a message, disconnects, or causes an error, respectively. It is within these four methods that the unique logic of your real-time application resides.

Let's begin by building the simplest possible example: a server that simply echoes back any message it receives. First, we'll create our application class. For a multi-user application, it's conventional to name this class after the concept it manages, such as `Chat`.

```php
<?php

// src/Chat.php


namespace App;


use Ratchet\MessageComponentInterface;

use Ratchet\ConnectionInterface;
```

```php
class Chat implements
MessageComponentInterface

{

    public function
onOpen(ConnectionInterface $conn)

    {

        // A new connection has been opened

        echo "New connection! ({$conn-
>resourceId})\n";

    }



    public function
onMessage(ConnectionInterface $from, $msg)

    {

        // A message was received from a
connection

        echo "Received message from {$from-
>resourceId}: {$msg}\n";



        // Echo the message back to the
sender

        $from->send($msg);

    }
```

```php
    public function
onClose(ConnectionInterface $conn)

    {

        // A connection has been closed

        echo "Connection {$conn->resourceId}
has disconnected\n";

    }



    public function
onError(ConnectionInterface $conn,
\Exception $e)

    {

        // An error has occurred

        echo "An error has occurred: {$e-
>getMessage()}\n";

        $conn->close();

    }

}
```

This class provides the core logic. Now we need a separate script to act as the server's entry point. This script will be responsible for instantiating all the Ratchet components, wrapping our Chat class, and starting the event loop. This is a long-running process that you will start from your command line.

```php
<?php

// server.php (in your project's root directory)


require dirname(__DIR__) . '/vendor/autoload.php';


use Ratchet\Server\IoServer;

use Ratchet\Http\HttpServer;

use Ratchet\WebSocket\WsServer;

use App\Chat;


// Create the server, wrapping our Chat application
$server = IoServer::factory(

    new HttpServer(

        new WsServer(

            new Chat()

        )

    ),
```

```
    8080 // The port to listen on

);


echo "WebSocket server started on port
8080\n";


// Start the event loop and run the server

$server->run();
```

To start our server, we run this script from the terminal: `php server.php`. Our server is now live, listening for connections on port 8080. The `run()` method starts the underlying ReactPHP event loop, and the script will now block, running indefinitely until it is manually stopped (e.g., with Ctrl+C).

While our echo server is a good start, it's not very social. The true power of WebSockets lies in facilitating communication between multiple users. Let's evolve our `Chat` class into a true multi-user broadcast system. To do this, we need a way to keep track of every single client that is currently connected to our server. A perfect tool for this is PHP's `SplObjectStorage`, a class that works like an array for objects, allowing us to attach and detach objects efficiently.

We'll modify our `Chat` class to maintain a list of connected clients. When a new connection is opened (`onOpen`), we'll add it to our list. When a connection is closed (`onClose`), we'll remove it. The most important change is in the `onMessage` method. When a message arrives from one client, we will now iterate over our entire list of connected clients and send that message to every single one of them.

```php
<?php

// src/Chat.php (updated for broadcasting)

namespace App;


use Ratchet\MessageComponentInterface;

use Ratchet\ConnectionInterface;


class Chat implements
MessageComponentInterface

{

    protected $clients;


    public function __construct()

    {

        $this->clients = new
\SplObjectStorage;

    }


    public function
onOpen(ConnectionInterface $conn)

    {
```

```php
        // Store the new connection to send
messages to later

        $this->clients->attach($conn);

        echo "New connection! ({$conn-
>resourceId})\n";

    }



    public function
onMessage(ConnectionInterface $from, $msg)

    {

        $numRecv = count($this->clients) -
1;

        echo sprintf('Connection %d sending
message "%s" to %d other connection%s' .
"\n",

            $from->resourceId, $msg,
$numRecv, $numRecv == 1 ? '' : 's');



        foreach ($this->clients as $client)
{

            // We want to broadcast the
message to everyone *except* the sender

            if ($from !== $client) {

                $client->send($msg);
```

```php
        }

    }

  }


    public function
onClose(ConnectionInterface $conn)

    {

        // The connection is closed, remove
it, as we can no longer send it messages

        $this->clients->detach($conn);

        echo "Connection {$conn->resourceId}
has disconnected\n";

    }



    public function
onError(ConnectionInterface $conn,
\Exception $e)

    {

        echo "An error has occurred: {$e-
>getMessage()}\n";

        $conn->close();

    }

}
```

With our server logic in place, we need a client to talk to it. The WebSocket API is a native part of all modern web browsers, making the client-side implementation surprisingly simple. The first step is to create a new `WebSocket` object in JavaScript, pointing it to our server's address. Note the use of the `ws://` protocol scheme (`wss://` for secure connections, the equivalent of HTTPS).

Once the `WebSocket` object is created, we can attach event listeners to it. These events, `onopen`, `onmessage`, `onclose`, and `onerror`, mirror their server-side counterparts perfectly. The `onopen` event fires when the handshake is successful and the connection is ready. The `onmessage` event fires every time a message arrives from the server; the message content is available in the `data` property of the event object. To send a message to the server, we simply call the `socket.send()` method.

Let's create a simple HTML file to act as our chat client. It will have an area to display messages, an input box to type them, and a button to send them.

```
<!DOCTYPE html>

<html>

<head>

    <title>Ratchet Chat</title>

</head>

<body>

    <ul id="messages"></ul>

    <form id="chat-form">
```

```html
    <input type="text" id="message-input" autocomplete="off" />

    <button>Send</button>

</form>


<script>

    const messagesList =
document.getElementById('messages');

    const chatForm =
document.getElementById('chat-form');

    const messageInput =
document.getElementById('message-input');


    // Establish the WebSocket
connection

    const socket = new
WebSocket('ws://localhost:8080');


    // Connection opened

    socket.onopen = function (e) {

        console.log("Connection
established!");

    };
```

```javascript
        // Listen for messages from the
server

        socket.onmessage = function (event)
{

            const li =
document.createElement('li');

            li.textContent = 'Received: ' +
event.data;

            messagesList.appendChild(li);

        };



        // Connection closed

        socket.onclose = function (event) {

            if (event.wasClean) {

                console.log(`Connection
closed cleanly, code=${event.code}
reason=${event.reason}`);

            } else {

                console.error('Connection
died');

            }

        };
```

```javascript
// Handle errors

socket.onerror = function (error) {

    console.error(`WebSocket Error:
${error.message}`);

};



// Send a message when the form is
submitted

chatForm.addEventListener('submit',
function (e) {

    e.preventDefault();

    if (messageInput.value) {

socket.send(messageInput.value);



        // Add our own message to
the list

        const li =
document.createElement('li');

        li.textContent = 'Sent: ' +
messageInput.value;


messagesList.appendChild(li);
```

```
                messageInput.value = '';

            }

        });

    </script>

</body>

</html>
```

If you restart your `server.php` script and open this HTML file in two separate browser tabs, you have a working chat application. A message typed into one tab will be sent to the PHP server, which will then broadcast it to the other tab, where it will appear almost instantly.

Our chat application is functional, but it's completely anonymous. A critical question remains: how do we tie a WebSocket connection to an authenticated user? The standard `Authorization: Bearer <token>` header cannot be sent after the initial handshake. The most common and widely accepted solution is to pass the user's authentication token (such as the JWT we created in Chapter 10) as a query string parameter in the WebSocket connection URL.

```
const socket = new
WebSocket('ws://localhost:8080?token=YOUR_JW
T_HERE');
```

This approach has security trade-offs—the token might be visible in server logs—but it is often the most pragmatic solution. On the server side, we need to intercept and validate this token during the HTTP handshake phase, before the connection is upgraded.

Ratchet's layered architecture makes this possible. We can create a simple middleware-like class that wraps our main `Chat` application. This wrapper's `onOpen` method will have access to the initial HTTP request object. It can inspect the query parameters, validate the JWT, and if it's valid, pass the connection on to the real chat application. If the token is invalid, it can simply close the connection immediately.

This authenticated connection allows us to build much richer applications. Instead of just broadcasting a raw message, we could prepend the authenticated user's name. In `onOpen`, we could store the user's name or ID on the connection object itself (e.g., `$conn->username = $decodedToken->username;`), making it available in the `onMessage` handler. This allows us to create private messaging, user-specific notifications, and a host of other real-time features that depend on a clear understanding of user identity.

As your real-time application grows in popularity, you will inevitably face the challenge of scaling. A single server can only handle a finite number of concurrent WebSocket connections. The obvious solution is to run multiple instances of your server behind a load balancer. However, this introduces a new problem. If User A is connected to Server 1 and User B is connected to Server 2, how does a message from User A get to User B? Server 1 knows nothing about the clients connected to Server 2.

The solution is to introduce a shared communication channel that all your WebSocket servers can access, often called a "backplane." A fantastic tool for this is Redis and its Publish/Subscribe (Pub/Sub) feature. In this architecture, when Server 1 receives a message from User A, it doesn't just send it to its own clients. It also publishes that message to a central Redis channel. Server 1, Server 2, and every other server instance are also subscribed to this same Redis channel. When the message arrives from Redis, each server receives it and then broadcasts it to its own local set of connected clients. This decouples the servers from each other, allowing you to scale horizontally by simply adding more server instances, all coordinated through the central message bus.

Finally, deploying a WebSocket server requires a different mindset than deploying a traditional web application. Because it is a long-running process, you cannot rely on PHP-FPM to manage it. You need a process control system, such as Supervisor, running on your server. Supervisor is a tool that will start your `server.php` script, monitor it to make sure it stays running, and automatically restart it if it ever crashes. This ensures that your real-time service is robust and available, ready to handle the constant, fluid stream of communication that defines the modern, interactive web.

CHAPTER FIFTEEN: Testing Methodologies: Unit, Integration, and End-to-End Testing

There is a moment in every developer's career, often arriving late at night before a major deadline, that marks a point of no return. It is the moment you fix a bug in one part of the application, only to discover with dawning horror that your "fix" has silently broken three other, seemingly unrelated features. This experience, a grim rite of passage, is the direct consequence of working without a safety net. In software development, that safety net is a comprehensive suite of automated tests. Writing tests is not a luxury reserved for projects with infinite time and budgets; it is a fundamental discipline of professional software engineering. It is the practice that transforms code from a fragile house of cards into a robust, resilient structure.

Tests are your application's first line of defense against itself. They are the tireless, automated sentinels that verify your code does what you think it does, and just as importantly, that it continues to do so as the application evolves. A good test suite allows you to refactor with courage, add new features with confidence, and upgrade dependencies without fear. It is a form of living documentation, demonstrating exactly how your code is intended to be used. This chapter is your introduction to this critical discipline. We will dissect the three primary layers of automated testing—unit, integration, and end-to-end—and explore the tools and techniques that allow us to build a robust safety net for our modern PHP applications.

A useful mental model for structuring a test suite is the "testing pyramid." Imagine a pyramid with three layers. The wide, sturdy base is made of **unit tests**. These are numerous, fast, and test tiny, isolated pieces of your code. The middle layer, smaller than the base, consists of **integration tests**. These are slower and more complex, and they verify that several of your application's components work correctly together. At the very peak of the pyramid is a small, sharp point made of **end-to-end tests**. These are the slowest and most brittle tests, but they provide the ultimate validation by simulating a real user's journey through the entire application, from the browser to the database and back again. A healthy, effective, and maintainable test suite respects the proportions of this pyramid.

The Foundation: Unit Testing

At the very base of the pyramid lies the unit test. A unit test is a small, automated test that verifies the behavior of a single, isolated "unit" of code. In the context of our object-oriented PHP applications, a unit is almost always a single class. The goal of a unit test is to prove that a specific method on a class behaves as expected given a certain set of inputs. To achieve this, a unit test must adhere to a strict rule: it must be completely isolated from its dependencies. This means a true unit test should never touch the database, the filesystem, the network, or any other external service. It is a test of the class's internal logic and nothing more.

This principle of isolation is what makes unit tests so fast and reliable. A suite of thousands of unit tests can often be run in a matter of seconds. Because they have no external dependencies, they are not flaky; a failing unit test points directly to a problem in the specific class under test, not to a network outage or a misconfigured database. The de facto standard tool for writing unit tests in the PHP ecosystem is PHPUnit. It is a mature, powerful, and feature-rich framework that provides the assertions and test-running capabilities we need. A more recent alternative, Pest, has gained significant popularity for its beautifully expressive and readable syntax, but it's important to know that under the hood, Pest is a cleverly designed layer on top of PHPUnit, so the core concepts are identical.

Let's write our first unit test. Imagine we have a simple Value Object from our application, designed to represent a price. Its logic ensures that a price can never be negative.

```php
<?php

// src/ValueObjects/Money.php

namespace App\ValueObjects;


class Money

{

    public function __construct(

        public readonly int $amount, //
Store money in cents to avoid float
inaccuracies

        public readonly string $currency,

    ) {

        if ($this->amount < 0) {

            throw new
\InvalidArgumentException('Amount cannot be
negative.');

        }

    }

}
```

To test this class, we would create a corresponding test file, typically in a tests/Unit directory. The test class will extend PHPUnit\Framework\TestCase, and each test is a public method that begins with the word test. A common and highly recommended pattern for structuring a test method is **Arrange-Act-Assert (AAA)**.

1. **Arrange**: Set up the world for your test. This involves instantiating objects and preparing any necessary data.

2. **Act**: Perform the single action that you are testing. This is usually a single method call on the object under test.

3. **Assert**: Make a claim about the outcome. This is where you verify that the action produced the expected result.

```php
<?php

// tests/Unit/MoneyTest.php

namespace Tests\Unit;


use App\ValueObjects\Money;

use PHPUnit\Framework\TestCase;


class MoneyTest extends TestCase
{

    public function test_it_can_be_instantiated_with_a_positive_amount(): void

    {

        // Arrange

        $amount = 1000; // 10.00 USD
```

```php
        $currency = 'USD';


        // Act

        $money = new Money($amount,
$currency);



        // Assert

        $this->assertSame($amount, $money-
>amount);

        $this->assertSame($currency, $money-
>currency);

    }



    public function
test_it_throws_an_exception_for_a_negative_a
mount(): void

    {

        // Arrange

        $this-
>expectException(\InvalidArgumentException::
class);



        // Act & Assert (combined in this
case)
```

```php
        new Money(-500, 'USD');

    }

}
```

In the first test, we simply assert that after creating the object, its properties hold the correct values. PHPUnit provides a rich library of assertion methods, like `assertSame`, `assertEquals`, `assertTrue`, and `assertCount`, to check for various conditions. The second test is equally important; it verifies our business rule that a negative amount is not allowed. The `$this->expectException()` method tells PHPUnit that this test is expected to throw a specific type of exception. The test will only pass if that exact exception is thrown during its execution.

This is straightforward for a self-contained class, but what about a class with dependencies? Consider our `TaskController` from Chapter 8, which depends on a `TaskRepository`. If we were to test the controller directly, it would try to talk to the repository, which would in turn try to talk to the database. This would violate the core principle of a unit test. The solution is to use **test doubles**, often referred to as **mocks**. A mock is a fake object that we create for the purpose of the test. It impersonates the real dependency, allowing us to control its behavior and make assertions about how it was used.

This is where the power of Dependency Injection becomes crystal clear. Because our controller receives its dependencies in the constructor, we can easily pass it a fake `TaskRepository` during a test.

```php
<?php

// tests/Unit/TaskControllerTest.php
```

```php
class TaskControllerTest extends TestCase
{
    public function
test_get_task_returns_task_data_when_found()
: void

    {

        // Arrange


        // 1. Create a mock of the
TaskRepository.

        $repositoryMock = $this-
>createMock(TaskRepository::class);


        $taskData = ['id' => 1, 'user_id' =>
1, 'title' => 'Test Task'];


        // 2. Configure the mock. Tell it
that when its `findById` method

        // is called with the argument `1`,
it should return our fake task data.

        $repositoryMock->expects($this-
>once())

                ->method('findById')
```

```php
            ->with(1)

            -
>willReturn($taskData);


        // 3. Instantiate the controller
with the mock repository.

        $controller = new
TaskController($repositoryMock);


        // We also need mock Request and
Response objects for the controller method.

        $request = $this-
>createMock(Request::class);

        $response = new Response();

        $args = ['id' => 1];


        // Act

        $actualResponse = $controller-
>getTask($request, $response, $args);


        // Assert

        $this->assertSame(200,
$actualResponse->getStatusCode());
```

```
        $this-
>assertJsonStringEqualsJsonString(

            json_encode($taskData),

            (string) $actualResponse-
>getBody()

        );

    }

}
```

In this test, we have completely isolated the `TaskController`.
We are testing its logic—that it correctly calls the repository and
formats the response—without ever touching the database. The
`createMock()` method from PHPUnit creates our fake
repository. We then use methods like `expects()`, `method()`,
and `willReturn()` to program its behavior for this specific test.
This level of control allows us to test every possible scenario,
including edge cases like what happens when the repository
returns `null`, all without the slowness and complexity of setting
up a real database.

The Middle Ground: Integration Testing

While unit tests are essential for verifying the logic of individual
classes, they cannot tell you if those classes actually work together
correctly. Does your `PdoTaskRepository` correctly interpret
the data from your MySQL database? Does your DI container
correctly assemble your `TaskController` with a real
repository? Answering these questions is the job of integration
tests. An integration test verifies the interaction, or "integration,"
between two or more components of your system. Unlike unit
tests, they are allowed to cross boundaries and interact with
external services like a database or a caching layer.

The most common and valuable type of integration test for a web application is the one that tests the path from your data access layer (the Repository or ORM) to the database. This test verifies that your SQL queries are correct, your table mappings are right, and your data is being persisted and retrieved as you expect. Because these tests interact with a real database, they are inherently slower and more complex to set up than unit tests.

The first requirement for integration testing is a dedicated testing database. You should never run your tests against your development or production databases. A common strategy is to use an in-memory database like SQLite for speed during testing, or to have a separate, dedicated database (e.g., `my_app_test`) on your database server. Before each test run, this database needs to be in a clean, known state. This is often achieved by running your database migrations to create the schema and then, between each individual test, using a strategy to isolate the data. The most common approach is to wrap each test method in a database transaction. The test starts a transaction, inserts any data it needs, performs its actions, and then, at the end of the test, the transaction is rolled back, leaving the database completely clean for the next test.

Let's write an integration test for our `PdoTaskRepository`. This test will extend the PHPUnit `TestCase` just like our unit tests, but it will include setup logic to establish a real database connection.

```php
<?php

// tests/Integration/PdoTaskRepositoryTest.php

namespace Tests\Integration;


use App\Repositories\PdoTaskRepository;
```

```php
use PDO;

use PHPUnit\Framework\TestCase;


class PdoTaskRepositoryTest extends TestCase
{
    private PDO $pdo;

    private PdoTaskRepository $repository;


    // This method is called by PHPUnit
    before each test method is run.

    protected function setUp(): void

    {
        // 1. Establish a connection to a
        test database (e.g., an in-memory SQLite).

        $this->pdo = new
        PDO('sqlite::memory:');

        // 2. Set up the necessary table
        schema.

        $this->pdo->exec("CREATE TABLE tasks
        (

            id INTEGER PRIMARY KEY,

            user_id INTEGER,
```

```php
        title TEXT,

        completed BOOLEAN

    )");

    // 3. Begin a transaction.

    $this->pdo->beginTransaction();


    $this->repository = new
PdoTaskRepository($this->pdo);

    }


    // This method is called after each test
method.

    protected function tearDown(): void

    {

        // 4. Roll back the transaction to
clean up.

        $this->pdo->rollBack();

    }


    public function
test_find_by_id_returns_task_when_it_exists(
): void
```

```
    {

        // Arrange

        // Insert a known record directly
into the test database.

        $this->pdo->exec("INSERT INTO tasks
(id, user_id, title, completed)

                          VALUES (1, 1,
'Integration Test Task', 0)");


        // Act

        $result = $this->repository-
>findById(1);


        // Assert

        $this->assertIsArray($result);

        $this->assertSame('Integration Test
Task', $result['title']);

    }

}
```

This test gives us a much higher level of confidence than a unit test alone. It proves that the SQL query inside our findById method is syntactically correct and that it correctly retrieves and formats data from a real database environment. This is the second layer of our safety net.

The Peak of the Pyramid: End-to-End Testing

At the very top of the pyramid are end-to-end (E2E) tests. An E2E test, also known as a browser test or functional test, simulates a complete user journey through your application from start to finish. It automates a real web browser (like Chrome or Firefox), instructing it to navigate to your application's URL, click on links, fill out forms, and assert that the content on the page is what it should be. This is the ultimate validation, as it tests your entire technology stack working in concert: the frontend HTML and CSS, the client-side JavaScript, your web server configuration, your PHP framework's routing and controllers, your business logic, and the database.

Because they involve the overhead of a real browser and simulate a user's comparatively slow interaction, E2E tests are by far the slowest and most resource-intensive type of test. They are also the most brittle. A small change in a CSS selector or a piece of JavaScript can easily break an E2E test, even if the underlying functionality of the application is still correct. For these reasons, E2E tests should be used sparingly. You do not write an E2E test for every possible scenario. Instead, you reserve them for the most critical, high-level user flows in your application, often called the "happy paths." These are the journeys that are absolutely essential for your application to function, such as the user registration process, the login flow, or the core checkout process in an e-commerce site.

Writing and running E2E tests requires a specialized set of tools. The classic tool for browser automation is Selenium, which provides a way to remotely control a browser. However, modern PHP frameworks often provide more integrated and developer-friendly solutions. The most prominent example is Laravel Dusk, which provides an expressive API for browser testing built on top of ChromeDriver. Even without a full-stack framework, you can use libraries like Panther (a standalone component from the Symfony ecosystem) or frameworks like Codeception to write and run these tests.

Let's outline the steps for a hypothetical E2E test of our user registration flow. The code for this is highly dependent on the specific testing tool, but the logical steps are universal.

- **Start with a clean slate**: Ensure the test database is in a known, empty state.

- **Launch the browser**: The test runner programmatically opens a new Chrome window.

- **Navigate to the registration page**: Instruct the browser to visit `http://localhost:8000/register`.

- **Interact with the form**:

   o Find the input field with the name `username` and type "John Doe".

   o Find the input field with the name `email` and type "john@example.com".

   o Find the input field for the password and type "password123".

- **Submit the form**: Find the "Register" button and programmatically click it.

- **Assert the outcome**:

   o The test framework waits for the browser to be redirected.

   o Assert that the new URL is `http://localhost:8000/login`.

   o Assert that the page contains the text "Registration successful. Please log in."

- **Verify the side effect**:

o The test can now go beyond the browser and directly query the test database.

o Assert that a `users` table now contains a row with the email "john@example.com".

A single test like this provides an enormous amount of confidence. It proves that your routing is correct, your controller can accept form data, your validation passes with valid input, your `password_hash` function is working, your user repository can insert a record, and your Post-Redirect-Get pattern is implemented correctly. It is the ultimate confirmation that the core pieces of your application are wired together and functioning as a cohesive whole.

A robust testing strategy employs all three types of tests in the proportions suggested by the pyramid. The vast majority of your logic will be covered by hundreds or thousands of lightning-fast unit tests. A smaller, more focused set of integration tests will ensure that your application's most important components can talk to each other and to external services like the database. Finally, a handful of carefully chosen E2E tests will guard your most critical user journeys. This multi-layered approach provides the best balance of confidence, speed, and maintainability. In the next chapters, we will see how to take this suite of automated tests and integrate it into a Continuous Integration pipeline, creating a system that automatically verifies the health of your application every single time you make a change, transforming your safety net into an automated, ever-vigilant guardian of your code's quality.

CHAPTER SIXTEEN: Caching Strategies for High Performance

In the world of web applications, speed is not just a feature; it is the feature. Users have grown to expect instantaneous responses, and a delay of even a few hundred milliseconds can be the difference between a happy, engaged user and a frustrated one who clicks away to a competitor. As developers, we spend a great deal of time optimizing our code, writing efficient database queries, and designing clean architectures. Yet, there comes a point where simply making the code run faster is not enough. The most powerful performance gains often come not from doing things faster, but from not doing them at all. This is the simple, profound philosophy behind caching.

A cache is a high-speed storage layer that stores a subset of data, typically transient in nature, so that future requests for that data are served up faster than is possible by accessing the data's primary storage location. In simpler terms, it's a temporary memory for the results of expensive work. If calculating a complex report takes five seconds of database queries, a cache allows us to perform that calculation once, store the resulting report, and for the next hour, serve that stored copy in a matter of milliseconds to every user who asks for it. It is an indispensable tool for building scalable, responsive, and cost-effective applications, reducing load on your servers, alleviating pressure on your database, and delivering a dramatically better experience to your end-users.

However, caching is not a magical solution you can sprinkle on an application to make it fast. It is a deliberate engineering trade-off. By choosing to serve a stored copy of data, you are inherently choosing to serve data that might be out of date. The core challenge of any caching strategy is managing this trade-off between performance and freshness. This leads to what is often called one of the two hard things in computer science: cache invalidation. Knowing when to intelligently remove stale data from the cache is the art and science that separates a simple caching implementation from a robust, high-performance one.

The Caching Pyramid: Layers of Performance

Before we dive into the code we write as PHP developers, it is crucial to understand that caching is not a monolithic concept. A modern web application is a complex stack of technologies, and performance optimizations can be applied at multiple layers. A well-architected system leverages caching at each of these layers, with each layer handling the type of content it is best suited for. This creates a multi-stage defense against slowness, where each layer attempts to serve the request before it needs to be passed on to the slower, more expensive layer below it.

At the very top, and closest to the user, is **Client-Side or Browser Caching**. This is the fastest cache of all because it completely avoids a network request. When a browser downloads a resource for the first time—like a CSS file, a JavaScript bundle, a logo, or a font—the server can include HTTP headers in the response that instruct the browser on how to cache it. The `Cache-Control` header is the modern standard for this, allowing the server to specify a `max-age` in seconds. For example, `Cache-Control: public, max-age=31536000` tells any browser or proxy that this resource can be safely stored and reused for one year without asking the server again. For assets that change infrequently, this is a massive performance win, reducing server load and making subsequent page loads feel instantaneous for the user.

One step down from the user's browser is the **Content Delivery Network (CDN)**. A CDN is a globally distributed network of proxy servers that caches content in locations geographically closer to your users. When a user in Tokyo requests an image from your application hosted in a data center in Ireland, a CDN can serve a cached copy of that image from a server in Japan. This dramatically reduces network latency, which is often the single biggest factor in how fast a website feels. While primarily used for static assets like images and videos, CDNs can also be configured to cache entire HTML pages, offloading a tremendous amount of traffic from your origin server.

The final layer, and the one we have the most direct control over in our PHP code, is **Application-Level Caching**. This happens on our server, within our application's logic. This is where we store the results of dynamic operations that are expensive to generate. These might include the results of complex database queries, the data fetched from slow third-party APIs, or even pre-rendered fragments of HTML. It is this layer that we will focus on for the remainder of the chapter, as it is where our strategic decisions as developers can have the most profound impact on the application's performance and scalability.

The Tools of the Trade: Caching Backends

When our PHP application decides to cache a piece of data, it needs a place to store it. This storage system is known as the cache backend or cache store. While it's possible to use the filesystem, this approach is generally slow and becomes a synchronization nightmare in a multi-server environment. For professional applications, the choice almost always comes down to dedicated in-memory data stores, which are purpose-built for the extreme speed that caching demands.

The two dominant players in this space are Memcached and Redis. **Memcached** is the very definition of a pure cache. It is a simple, incredibly fast, distributed in-memory key-value store. You give it a key and a value, and it stores it in RAM. Later, you ask for the key, and you get the value back at lightning speed. It is volatile by nature; if a Memcached server restarts, all of its cached data is gone, which is perfectly acceptable for its intended purpose as a temporary store.

Redis, on the other hand, is often described as a data structure server. While it is an outstandingly fast in-memory key-value store and is frequently used as a cache, its capabilities extend far beyond that. Redis supports a rich set of data structures, such as lists, sets, hashes, and sorted sets, directly on the server. It can also be

246

configured for persistence, writing its data to disk to survive restarts. This versatility means Redis is often used not just for caching, but also for session management, job queues, and real-time messaging with its Pub/Sub features. For most new projects, Redis is the more powerful and flexible choice, but the simplicity and focused nature of Memcached still make it a viable option.

Before we even get to these dedicated services, it is worth mentioning **Opcode Caching**. This is a special, low-level type of cache that is a standard feature of modern PHP, known as OPcache. When a PHP script is executed, the interpreter first has to parse the human-readable code into a set of machine-understandable instructions called opcodes. OPcache works by storing these pre-compiled opcodes in shared memory. The next time that same script is requested, the interpreter can skip the entire compilation step and execute the cached opcodes directly. This provides a massive performance boost with zero changes to your application code. OPcache is enabled by default in most modern PHP installations, and for any production server, ensuring it is enabled and properly configured is the single most effective performance optimization you can make.

A Common Language: PSR-6 and PSR-16

To prevent developers from being tightly coupled to a specific caching library or backend, the PHP-FIG has established two standard interfaces for interacting with caches: PSR-6 and PSR-16. These standards allow us to write our application logic against a common interface, and then, with a simple configuration change, swap out the underlying implementation—from a simple file-based cache in development to a powerful Redis cluster in production.

PSR-16 (Simple Cache) provides a straightforward, easy-to-use interface for the most common caching operations. It is the interface you will likely interact with most often in your application code. It defines a `CacheInterface` with a handful of intuitive methods: `get($key)`, `set($key, $value, $ttl)`, `delete($key)`, and `has($key)`. The `$ttl` (Time

To Live) argument specifies how long the item should be kept in the cache, either in seconds or as a `DateInterval` object. This simple contract is all that is needed for the vast majority of application-level caching tasks.

PSR-6 (Caching Interface) is a more advanced and powerful standard, but it is also more verbose. It is designed to give library authors finer-grained control over the caching process. Instead of working directly with values, you work with `CacheItemInterface` objects, which wrap the value and provide access to more metadata, such as expiration timestamps and tags. While powerful, its complexity is often unnecessary for typical application code. For our practical examples, we will focus on the clean and pragmatic PSR-16 interface.

The Cache-Aside Pattern: A Practical Implementation

The most common caching strategy you will implement is a pattern known as "Cache-Aside" or "Lazy Loading." The logic is simple and can be applied to any expensive operation. When your application needs a piece of data, it follows these steps:

1. Ask the cache for the data using a unique key.

2. If the cache has the data (a "cache hit"), return it immediately. The expensive operation is skipped.

3. If the cache does not have the data (a "cache miss"), then:

   a. Perform the expensive operation (e.g., query the database) to get the data.

   b. Store the result of that operation in the cache with the same unique key and a defined TTL.

   c. Return the data to the application.

Subsequent requests for the same data within the TTL period will now result in a cache hit. Let's see this in action. Imagine we have a dashboard page that needs to display some complex user statistics, a query that we don't want to run on every single page load. We can encapsulate this logic within our `UserRepository`. First, we'll install a PSR-16 compliant caching library that can talk to a backend like Redis. A popular choice is the caching component from the Symfony framework.

```
composer require symfony/cache
```

Now, we can update our DI container to configure a cache pool that connects to Redis and make it available for injection. The `symfony/cache` library provides an "adapter" that makes a PSR-6 cache pool compatible with the simpler PSR-16 interface.

```php
<?php

// bootstrap/container.php

use Psr\SimpleCache\CacheInterface;

use Symfony\Component\Cache\Adapter\RedisAdapter;

use Symfony\Component\Cache\Psr16Cache;



// ...

$containerBuilder->addDefinitions([

    // ...

    CacheInterface::class => function () {

        $redisClient =
RedisAdapter::createConnection('redis://localhost');
```

```php
        $psr6CachePool = new
RedisAdapter($redisClient);

        // Wrap the powerful PSR-6 pool with
the simple PSR-16 interface.

        return new
Psr16Cache($psr6CachePool);

    },

]);
```

With this in place, we can now inject CacheInterface into any class that needs it, such as our UserRepository. The repository can now implement the Cache-Aside pattern, completely transparently to the controller that calls it.

```php
<?php

// src/Repositories/UserRepository.php

namespace App\Repositories;


use PDO;

use Psr\SimpleCache\CacheInterface;


class UserRepository

{

    public function __construct(
```

```php
        private PDO $pdo,

        private CacheInterface $cache

    ) {}


    public function getUserStats(int $userId): array

    {

        // 1. Define a unique key for this piece of data.

        $cacheKey = "user.{$userId}.stats";


        // 2. Ask the cache for the data.

        $cachedStats = $this->cache->get($cacheKey);


        if ($cachedStats !== null) {

            // Cache Hit! The data was found in the cache.

            echo "<!-- CACHE HIT -->"; // For debugging

            return $cachedStats;

        }
```

```php
        // Cache Miss. The data was not in
the cache.

        echo "<!-- CACHE MISS -->"; // For
debugging



        // 3a. Perform the expensive
operation.

        // (This is a placeholder for a very
complex query)

        $stmt = $this->pdo->prepare("SELECT
COUNT(*) as post_count, SUM(views) as
total_views FROM posts WHERE user_id =
:id");

        $stmt->execute(['id' => $userId]);

        $stats = $stmt->fetch();



        // 3b. Store the result in the cache
with a TTL of 1 hour (3600 seconds).

        $this->cache->set($cacheKey, $stats,
3600);



        // 3c. Return the newly fetched
data.
```

```
        return $stats;

    }

}
```

When the `getUserStats` method is called for the first time, it will miss the cache, run the query, store the result, and return it. For the next hour, every subsequent call to that same method for the same user will hit the cache and return the stored data in microseconds, without ever touching the database. We have successfully traded absolute data freshness for a massive gain in performance.

The Hard Part: Cache Invalidation

Our Time-To-Live (TTL) based caching works wonderfully for data that can tolerate being a little stale. But what about data that must be updated immediately? If a user changes their username, we can't wait an hour for their old username to expire from every cache where it might be stored. This is where we need a strategy for explicit cache invalidation.

The most direct approach is to manually delete the cache key whenever the underlying data changes. In our user example, the method that handles updating the user's profile in the database would be responsible for also telling the cache to delete the corresponding entry.

```php
<?php

// Inside a UserService or UserRepository

public function updateUserProfile(int $userId, array $data): void

{
```

```
    // ... logic to update the user in the
database ...


    // After the database is successfully
updated, invalidate the cache.

    $cacheKey = "user.{$userId}.profile";

    $this->cache->delete($cacheKey);

}
```

This ensures that the next time the user's profile is requested, it will be a cache miss, and the fresh data will be fetched from the database and re-cached. This works well for simple cases, but it can quickly become complex. A single change might affect multiple cached items. For example, updating a product's name might require invalidating not only the product's own cache entry (product:123) but also the cache for several category pages (category:electronics:page:1), the homepage's "featured products" list (homepage:featured), and a user's list of recently viewed items (user:456:viewed). Manually tracking and deleting all these keys is tedious and highly error-prone.

A more advanced and robust solution to this problem is **Tag-Based Invalidation**. This powerful technique, supported by many PSR-6 compatible libraries and backends like Redis, allows you to associate one or more string tags with each cached item. Instead of just deleting items by their specific key, you can invalidate all items that share a common tag.

Let's revisit our product example. When we cache the homepage, which contains information about products 123 and 456, we would cache it with the tags product:123 and product:456. When we cache the electronics category page, we might tag it with

`product:123`, `product:789`, and
`category:electronics`. Now, when the name of product
123 is updated, we don't need to know every single key where that
product appears. We simply issue a single command: "invalidate
the tag `product:123`." The cache system will then find and
remove all items associated with that tag—the homepage and the
category page—in one atomic operation. This decouples our write
logic from our read logic, creating a much more maintainable and
scalable caching strategy.

Caching Best Practices

As you integrate caching into your application, there are several
key principles to keep in mind. First, **cache the right things**.
Caching is for data that is expensive to generate and is read
frequently. Don't waste time and memory caching things that are
trivial to compute. Second, **use a consistent keying strategy**. A
clean, predictable naming scheme for your cache keys, such as
`object:id:field` (e.g., `user:123:profile`), will prevent
key collisions and make debugging vastly easier.

Third, **be mindful of what you store**. Caching complex PHP
objects can sometimes lead to issues, as they must be serialized
before being stored and unserialized upon retrieval. It is often
more robust to cache simple data structures like associative arrays
and then use that data to construct your objects. Finally, **handle
cache failures gracefully**. Your cache server is an external
dependency; it could become unavailable. Your code should be
written defensively so that if the cache fails, it can fall back to
fetching the data from the primary source. The application might
get slower, but it should not crash entirely. Caching is an
optimization, not a hard requirement for your application's core
logic to function. By thoughtfully applying these strategies, you
can transform a sluggish application into a high-performance,
scalable system capable of handling immense traffic while feeling
responsive and immediate to every user.

CHAPTER SEVENTEEN: Securing Your Application Against Common Threats

We have constructed an application with a logical architecture, a persistent memory, and an interactive face. We have taught it to identify its users and respect their ownership of data. In doing so, we have laid a solid foundation. But on the web, a solid foundation is not enough. The internet, for all its wonders, is an inherently hostile environment. Malicious actors, automated bots, and curious tinkerers are constantly probing for weaknesses, seeking to exploit the smallest oversight. Security is not a feature you add at the end of a project, like a coat of paint. It is a continuous process, a mindset of disciplined paranoia that must be woven into every line of code you write and every component you deploy. It is the practice of building not just a house, but a fortress.

In previous chapters, we have already laid some of the essential security groundwork. We know to use prepared statements to prevent SQL Injection, to escape our output to thwart Cross-Site Scripting (XSS), and to use CSRF tokens to protect our forms. These are the load-bearing walls of our fortress. This chapter is about reinforcing the perimeter. We will move beyond the most well-known vulnerabilities and explore a broader range of common threats, from the dangers lurking in an innocent file upload to the subtle misconfigurations that can expose your entire system. The goal is to cultivate a "defense in depth" strategy, where multiple layers of security work in concert to protect your application and, most importantly, the trust of your users.

The Dangers of Generosity: File Upload Vulnerabilities

Allowing users to upload files is a common requirement for countless applications, from social media sites needing profile pictures to business applications handling invoices. It is also one of the most dangerous features you can implement. When you accept a file from a user, you are inviting a piece of the unknown internet onto your server. If not handled with extreme care, a seemingly innocuous image upload could become a backdoor, allowing an attacker to execute arbitrary code and take complete control of your system.

The most catastrophic vulnerability is unrestricted file execution. Imagine an attacker renames a malicious PHP script from `shell.php` to `shell.php.jpg` and uploads it as their profile picture. A naive validation check that only looks at the file extension might be fooled into thinking it's a harmless image. If that file is then stored in a publicly accessible web directory (like `/uploads/avatars/`), the attacker can simply navigate to `https://example.com/uploads/avatars/shell.php.jpg`. If the web server is configured to execute files based on its interpretation rather than just the extension (which some configurations might do), or if the attacker can find a way to trick the server into including the file, the PHP script will execute, and the game is over.

To properly secure file uploads, you must implement a strict, multi-layered validation and storage strategy. First, never trust the filename, file size, or MIME type provided by the client. All of this information can be easily faked. Your server-side code must be the sole arbiter of what is acceptable. When a file is uploaded, PHP stores it in a temporary location. Your first job is to inspect this temporary file. Use PHP's Fileinfo functions, specifically `finfo_file`, to determine the file's true MIME type based on its actual binary content. This provides a much more reliable check than the user-supplied `$_FILES['upload']['type']`. You should maintain an explicit "allow list" of acceptable MIME types (e.g., `image/jpeg`, `image/png`, `application/pdf`) and reject anything not on that list.

Second, upon successful validation, you must never store the file using its original, user-supplied filename. This name could contain malicious characters designed to perform directory traversal attacks (e.g., `../../evil.php`) or simply be crafted to cause conflicts. The best practice is to generate a new, unique, and random filename for the uploaded content. A good strategy is to combine a hash of the file's contents with a timestamp or a universally unique identifier (UUID). Store the original filename in the database if you need to display it to the user later.

Third, and this is the most critical rule: **store uploaded files outside of the web root directory**. Your web root is the `public` directory, the only folder that should be directly accessible via a URL. If your files are stored in, for example, a `storage/` directory at the same level as your `src/` and `vendor/` directories, there is no URL an attacker can type into their browser to execute it. This single architectural decision eliminates the risk of direct execution. To serve these private files to legitimate users, you must create a dedicated PHP script or controller action. This script acts as a secure gatekeeper. It would receive a request for a file (e.g., `/files/download/{fileId}`), perform any necessary authorization checks to ensure the current user is allowed to access that file, fetch the file from its secure storage location on the disk, and then stream it to the user's browser with the correct `Content-Type` header. This approach gives you complete control over file access and renders direct execution attacks impossible.

The Unlocked Door: Insecure Direct Object References (IDOR)

One of the most common and often overlooked vulnerabilities is a flaw in authorization, known as an Insecure Direct Object Reference, or IDOR. This occurs when an application provides direct access to objects based on user-supplied input, without first verifying that the user is actually authorized to access that specific object. It is the digital equivalent of a building where your key opens not just your own apartment, but every apartment on your floor if you just try it on their doors.

We touched on the core principle of this in Chapter 10 when we checked if a task's `user_id` matched the authenticated user's ID. IDOR is the formal name for the vulnerability that arises when this check is forgotten. Consider a URL like `https://example.com/invoices/view/101`. A user is authenticated, and the application correctly fetches the invoice with the ID 101 from the database and displays it. The vulnerability lies in what happens if the user, out of curiosity or malice, changes the URL to `https://example.com/invoices/view/102`. If the application's only logic is to `SELECT * FROM invoices WHERE id = 102`, it will happily fetch and display invoice 102, regardless of whether it belongs to the currently logged-in user. The attacker can now write a simple script to iterate through every possible ID, downloading every invoice in the system.

The fix for IDOR is conceptually simple but requires unwavering discipline: **for every single request that accesses a resource, you must perform an ownership check.** Your database query should never just ask "does this object exist?"; it must ask "does this object exist *and* does it belong to the current user?".

A typical query to fetch a resource should almost always include a `WHERE` clause that scopes the search to the authenticated user.

```php
<?php

// Inside a controller action

$invoiceId = (int) $args['id'];

$currentUserId = $request->getAttribute('userId'); // From our auth middleware

// The WRONG way (vulnerable to IDOR)

// $stmt = $this->pdo->prepare("SELECT * FROM invoices WHERE id = :id");

// $stmt->execute(['id' => $invoiceId]);

// The CORRECT way (scoped to the user)
```

```php
$sql = "SELECT * FROM invoices WHERE id =
:id AND user_id = :user_id";

$stmt = $this->pdo->prepare($sql);

$stmt->execute(['id' => $invoiceId,
'user_id' => $currentUserId]);

$invoice = $stmt->fetch();

if (!$invoice) {

// Return a 404 Not Found. Crucially, do not
return a 403 Forbidden.

// Doing so would leak the information that
the resource *exists*,

// but the user just doesn't have access to
it.

return $response->withStatus(404);

}

// ... proceed with displaying the invoice

?>
```

A subtle but important point is to return a 404 Not Found response even if the object exists but belongs to another user. This prevents an attacker from "information fishing" to determine which object IDs are valid. As far as the user is concerned, if they aren't allowed to see it, it might as well not exist. While using non-sequential, hard-to-guess identifiers like UUIDs instead of auto-incrementing integers can make it more difficult for an attacker to enumerate resources, this is a form of security by obscurity and is not a substitute for proper authorization checks. The ownership check is mandatory.

The Unkempt Workshop: Security Misconfiguration

Some of the most damaging security breaches are not the result of a clever, novel attack, but of a simple, preventable misconfiguration. These vulnerabilities are the unlocked windows and propped-open doors of your application's fortress. They often stem from using default settings, deploying verbose error messages to production, or failing to maintain the software components that make up your application.

One of the most common misconfigurations is the exposure of detailed error messages in a production environment. During development, seeing a full stack trace when an exception occurs is incredibly helpful for debugging. In production, it is a goldmine for an attacker. A detailed error message can leak critical information about your system: the internal directory structure of your server, the names and versions of the frameworks and libraries you are using, snippets of your source code, and even database query details. To prevent this, your production `php.ini` file must have `display_errors` set to `Off`. Errors should still be logged, but they should be written to a secure file on the server or sent to a dedicated logging service, never displayed to the user. Your framework should be configured with a generic, user-friendly error page that reveals nothing about the underlying cause of the failure.

Another critical area is dependency management. Our applications are built on the shoulders of open-source giants; our `vendor` directory is filled with third-party code. This is a huge productivity boost, but it also means we inherit any security vulnerabilities present in those packages. The `composer.lock` file ensures we have a consistent set of dependencies, but it doesn't ensure they are secure. Security vulnerabilities are discovered in popular libraries all the time. Failing to update your dependencies is like knowing there is a recall on your car's brakes but continuing to drive it. You must make it a regular practice to check for known vulnerabilities. The command `composer audit` is a built-in tool that checks your installed packages against a public database of known security advisories and will alert you to any dependencies that need to be updated. Integrating this check into your development and deployment workflow is a simple and highly effective way to protect your application from a vast range of known exploits.

Guarding the Gates: Hardening Authentication

Chapter 10 laid the groundwork for a secure authentication system using JWTs. However, the implementation of an authentication system is fertile ground for subtle but serious vulnerabilities. One of the most critical aspects is the security of the secret key used to sign the JWTs. This key is the ultimate source of trust in your token system. If an attacker can guess or obtain this key, they can forge valid tokens for any user, including administrators, and gain complete control of your application. Your secret key must be long, random, and completely unpredictable. It should never be a simple string like "secret" or the name of your application. Use a cryptographically secure random number generator to create a long string of characters.

Furthermore, this secret key must never be committed to your version control system (like Git). Your code is often more public than you think, and committing secrets is a recipe for disaster. The standard practice is to store secrets and other configuration that varies by environment (development, staging, production) in environment variables. Libraries like `vlucas/phpdotenv` allow you to manage these variables in a `.env` file at the root of your project. This `.env` file is then added to your `.gitignore` to ensure it is never committed. Your application code then reads the secret key from the environment at runtime.

Another challenge with the stateless nature of JWTs is token revocation. What happens if a user's token is stolen, or if a user explicitly logs out? By default, a JWT is valid until its expiration time (`exp` claim) is reached. To handle immediate invalidation, you must introduce a small amount of state back into your system. A common strategy is to maintain a "deny list" or "blocklist" of revoked tokens. This list can be stored in a fast data store like

Redis. When a user logs out, you add the unique identifier of their token (the `jti` claim) to this list, with an expiration set to match the token's original expiration time. Your authentication middleware must then be modified to perform an additional check: after successfully verifying the token's signature, it must also check if the token's ID exists in the deny list. If it does, the request is rejected. This provides a clean mechanism for instantly revoking credentials without sacrificing the primary benefits of a token-based system.

Instructing the Browser: HTTP Security Headers

The security of your application doesn't end when the response leaves your server. The modern web browser is an incredibly complex piece of software, and it can be instructed to enable powerful, built-in security features that can protect your users from a range of client-side attacks. These instructions are delivered via HTTP response headers. A few simple headers, added by a middleware in your application, can dramatically harden your application's client-side security posture.

The **Content-Security-Policy (CSP)** header is a powerful defense against XSS. It allows you to specify a strict "allow list" of sources from which the browser is permitted to load content, such as scripts, styles, images, and fonts. For example, you can tell the browser to only execute JavaScript files that come from your own domain and a trusted CDN. If an attacker manages to inject a malicious `<script src="https://evil.com/malware.js">` tag into your page, a browser that supports CSP will simply refuse to load and execute the script because `evil.com` is not on the allow list. Crafting a good CSP can be complex, but it provides a critical layer of defense.

HTTP Strict-Transport-Security (HSTS) is a header that instructs the browser to only ever communicate with your site over a secure HTTPS connection. After a browser sees this header for the first time, it will automatically turn any future insecure requests (`http://`) into secure ones (`https://`) before they are even sent. This prevents man-in-the-middle attacks where an attacker on an insecure network tries to downgrade the user's connection to plain HTTP to eavesdrop on their traffic.

Finally, headers like `X-Frame-Options` or the more modern `Content-Security-Policy: frame-ancestors 'self'` are used to prevent an attack called **clickjacking**. In a clickjacking attack, a malicious site loads your application in a transparent `<iframe>` overlaid on top of an innocuous-looking page. They might then trick the user into clicking what they think is a button on the malicious site, but the click is actually passed through to a button in your invisible application, potentially causing the user to perform an unwanted action like deleting their account. By sending a header that denies other sites permission to frame your application, you can completely mitigate this threat. Implementing a middleware that adds these security headers to all of your application's responses is a simple and highly effective way to leverage the browser's own security features to protect your users.

CHAPTER EIGHTEEN: Containerizing Your Application with Docker

We have reached a pivotal moment in our application's journey. It has been architected, built, secured, and tested. It lives on our local machine, a pristine and perfectly configured environment where every component works in harmony. The problem, of course, is that our application is not destined to live on our machine forever. It must eventually move to a staging server, and then to a production server, and it must be set up on the machines of our fellow developers. This is where a notorious and deeply frustrating problem often emerges, a phrase that has caused more collective groans in development teams than perhaps any other: "But it works on my machine."

This problem arises from the subtle, invisible differences between environments. Your local machine might be running PHP 8.3.1, while the production server is on 8.3.0. You might have a specific version of a system library like ImageMagick installed that your colleague does not. The database on your macOS machine might have a default collation that differs from the one on the production Linux server. Each of these tiny discrepancies is a potential source of bugs, deployment failures, and wasted hours of debugging. For decades, developers have tried to solve this with detailed setup guides, provisioning scripts, and virtual machines, but each solution brought its own complexity and overhead. The modern, elegant, and universally adopted solution to this problem is containerization, and the undisputed king of containerization is Docker.

Containerization is a lightweight form of virtualization that allows you to package up an application with all of its dependencies—the code, the PHP runtime, the system libraries, the configuration files—into a single, standardized, and self-sufficient unit called a container. The magic of a container is that it will run the exact same way regardless of where it is deployed. It could be your laptop, a continuous integration server, or a cloud provider's virtual machine. If it runs in a container on your machine, it will run in a container anywhere else.

To understand the power of this, it is helpful to use the analogy of real-world shipping containers. Before their invention, shipping goods was a chaotic process. Goods of all shapes and sizes were loaded onto ships by hand, a slow and inefficient process. The standardized shipping container changed everything. It did not matter what was inside the box—electronics, grain, or automobiles—the box itself had standard dimensions and could be moved by any crane and loaded onto any ship or truck in the world. Docker does for software what the shipping container did for global trade. It provides a standard "box" for your application, abstracting away the specifics of the underlying machine.

This differs fundamentally from a traditional Virtual Machine (VM). A VM virtualizes the entire hardware stack, meaning each VM runs a complete, independent guest operating system on top of the host operating system. This is effective but heavy; each VM consumes a significant amount of disk space, memory, and startup time. Containers, by contrast, virtualize at the operating system level. They share the host machine's OS kernel but have their own isolated view of the filesystem, network, and process space. This makes them incredibly lightweight, fast to start, and allows you to run many more containers on a single host than you could VMs.

The Docker platform consists of a few core components that work together. The Docker Engine is the runtime, the underlying service that builds, runs, and manages containers. We interact with it through a command-line interface. The two most important concepts we work with are Images and Containers. An **Image** is a read-only blueprint. It is a snapshot of everything needed to run our application: an operating system filesystem, the application code, and all its dependencies. A **Container** is a live, running instance of an image. You can have many running containers all based on the same single image, just as you can build many houses from a single blueprint.

So, how do we create this blueprint for our PHP application? We do it by writing a set of instructions in a special text file named, simply, `Dockerfile`. A Dockerfile is a recipe. It specifies a starting point (a base image), and then lists a series of steps to follow to assemble our final application image. Let's build a practical `Dockerfile` for the API we've been working on, step by step. A typical web application requires at least two processes: the web server (like Nginx) and the PHP interpreter itself. We will create an image for our PHP application first.

Every `Dockerfile` must begin with a `FROM` instruction. This specifies the base image we want to build upon. We don't need to build an entire operating system from scratch; we can leverage the vast library of official, pre-built images available on Docker Hub. For a PHP application that will be run by a separate web server, the ideal choice is an official PHP image with the FPM (FastCGI Process Manager) SAPI.

```
# Use an official PHP FPM image as a parent
image

FROM php:8.3-fpm
```

Next, we need to install any system-level dependencies our application might need, as well as any required PHP extensions. Many PHP applications need extensions for database access (like `pdo_mysql`) or image manipulation (`gd`). The `RUN` instruction allows us to execute any command inside a temporary container during the image build process. We can use the standard Debian package manager, `apt-get`, and a handy helper script provided in the official PHP images, `docker-php-ext-install`, to set these up.

```
# Install system dependencies
```

```
RUN apt-get update && apt-get install -y \

    git \

    unzip \

    libzip-dev \

    libpng-dev \

    libjpeg62-turbo-dev \

    libfreetype6-dev \

    && rm -rf /var/lib/apt/lists/*


# Install PHP extensions

RUN docker-php-ext-install pdo_mysql zip
exif pcntl

RUN docker-php-ext-configure gd --with-
freetype --with-jpeg

RUN docker-php-ext-install gd
```

Now we need to get our application code into the image. First, we'll set a working directory inside the container's filesystem. This is where all subsequent commands will be executed. Then, we use the COPY instruction to copy our application files from our host machine into the image. A crucial part of a modern PHP workflow is Composer, so we'll copy our composer.json and composer.lock files first and run composer install. By copying these files separately from the rest of our application code, we can take advantage of Docker's layer caching. If our dependencies haven't changed, Docker can reuse the layer from a previous build, making subsequent builds much faster.

```
# Set the working directory

WORKDIR /var/www/html
```

```
# Copy Composer files and install
dependencies

COPY composer.json composer.lock ./

RUN curl -sS
https://getcomposer.org/installer | php -- -
-install-dir=/usr/local/bin --
filename=composer

RUN composer install --no-dev --optimize-
autoloader
```

```
# Copy the rest of the application code

COPY . .
```

Finally, we need to ensure the files have the correct permissions so the web server can read and write to them, and we specify the default command that should be run when a container is started from this image. For an FPM image, that command is simply php-fpm.

```
# Fix permissions

RUN chown -R www-data:www-data /var/www/html


# Expose port 9000 and start php-fpm server

EXPOSE 9000

CMD ["php-fpm"]
```

With this `Dockerfile` in our project's root directory, we can build our application image with a single command: `docker build -t my-app-php .`. Docker will execute each instruction in the file, creating a new layer for each step, and ultimately tag the final image with the name `my-app-php`. We now have a self-contained, portable blueprint of our application.

Of course, our PHP application cannot serve requests on its own. It needs a web server to handle incoming HTTP traffic and a database to store its data. This is where our single container model falls short. A modern application is a system of collaborating services, and we need a way to define and manage this system. This is the job of Docker Compose. Docker Compose is a tool for defining and running multi-container Docker applications. With a single YAML configuration file, `docker-compose.yml`, you can configure all of your application's services, networks, and volumes.

A `docker-compose.yml` file for our application would define three main services: one for our PHP application (which we'll call `app`), one for the Nginx web server (`web`), and one for our MariaDB database (`db`). This file becomes the single source of truth for our entire development environment.

Let's define our `app` service first. Instead of specifying an image, we can tell Docker Compose to `build` it using the `Dockerfile` we just created. We also use a `volume` to mount our local source code directory directly into the container. This is a game-changer for development. It means any change we make to a PHP file on our host machine is instantly reflected inside the container, allowing for a rapid, live-reloading development workflow without needing to rebuild the image for every code change.

```
services:

  app:

    build:

      context: .

      dockerfile: Dockerfile

    container_name: my-app-php

    volumes:

      - .:/var/www/html
```

Next, we define our `web` service. We'll use the official Nginx image from Docker Hub. The key is to configure this Nginx container to forward any requests for PHP files to our `app` container. We do this by mounting a custom Nginx configuration file from our local machine into the container. We also map port 8080 on our host machine to port 80 inside the container, so we can access our application in the browser at `http://localhost:8080`.

```
  web:
```

```
image: nginx:alpine

container_name: my-app-web

ports:

    - "8080:80"

volumes:

    - .:/var/www/html

    -
./docker/nginx/default.conf:/etc/nginx/conf.
d/default.conf
```

The custom `default.conf` file is the crucial piece of wiring. It tells Nginx to serve static files directly and to pass any requests ending in `.php` to the PHP-FPM process running in our `app` container. Docker Compose automatically sets up a network for our services, allowing the Nginx container to resolve the `app` service by its name.

```
# docker/nginx/default.conf

server {

    listen 80;

    index index.php index.html;

    root /var/www/html/public;


    location ~ \.php$ {
```

```nginx
        fastcgi_pass app:9000; # 'app' is
the service name from docker-compose.yml

        fastcgi_index index.php;

        include fastcgi_params;

        fastcgi_param SCRIPT_FILENAME
$document_root$fastcgi_script_name;

    }

}
```

Finally, we define our db service. We use an official MariaDB image and pass in environment variables to set the root password and create our application's database and user. The most critical part of this configuration is the volume. A container's filesystem is ephemeral; if you remove the container, its data is gone. For a database, this is obviously not acceptable. We use a named volume, db_data, to persist the database files on the host machine. Docker manages this volume, ensuring that even if we stop and remove the db container, our data will be safe and will be re-attached the next time we start the service.

```yaml
  db:

    image: mariadb:10.6

    container_name: my-app-db

    environment:

      MYSQL_ROOT_PASSWORD: rootpassword
```

```
      MYSQL_DATABASE: my_app_db

      MYSQL_USER: db_user

      MYSQL_PASSWORD: db_password

   volumes:

      - db_data:/var/lib/mysql


volumes:

  db_data:
```

With this complete `docker-compose.yml` file at the root of our project, our entire development environment is now codified. A new developer joining the team no longer needs a multi-page setup guide. They simply need to have Docker installed, check out the code, and run a single command in their terminal: `docker-compose up -d`. This command reads the YAML file, builds the custom PHP image if it doesn't exist, pulls the Nginx and MariaDB images, and starts all three containers in the background, networking them together. The entire application stack is up and running in a matter of minutes, perfectly and consistently replicated.

The daily workflow becomes remarkably simple. The `docker-compose up` command starts everything, and `docker-compose down` stops it. What if you need to run a command inside the container, like `composer install` after pulling new changes, or `phpunit` to run your test suite? You can get a shell inside a running container with the `exec` command: `docker-compose exec app bash`. This drops you into a command prompt inside the PHP container, with access to all your code and tools, as if you were SSH'd into a dedicated server.

As you prepare to move from development to production, your Docker setup will evolve. In a production `Dockerfile`, you would likely use a multi-stage build. The first stage, the "builder," would install all your build-time dependencies like Composer, run `composer install`, and then the second, final stage would start from a clean PHP image and `COPY` only the necessary application code and vendor directory from the builder stage. This results in a much smaller, more secure production image that doesn't contain unnecessary build tools.

Furthermore, while Docker Compose is fantastic for local development and even for simple, single-server deployments, orchestrating a complex, scalable, and resilient production environment often calls for a more powerful tool. This is the domain of container orchestrators like Kubernetes. An orchestrator handles tasks like automatically deploying your containers across a cluster of servers, scaling them up or down based on traffic, restarting them if they fail, and managing complex networking and storage. Chapter 22, which covers Continuous Integration and Deployment, and Chapter 24 on scaling will explore how these containerized building blocks become the foundation for a modern, automated, and scalable deployment pipeline. The principles you've learned here—defining your application's environment as code, creating portable images, and orchestrating services—are the fundamental skills for deploying modern web applications in any environment.

CHAPTER NINETEEN: Interacting with Third-Party APIs and Services

No modern web application is an island. The days of building monolithic systems that attempt to do everything themselves are long gone. The contemporary software landscape is an interconnected ecosystem, a vibrant digital city where specialized services offer their expertise for a small fee or a simple API call. Need to process a credit card payment? There's an API for that. Need to send a transactional email or an SMS message? There's an API for that. Need to get the current weather, translate a block of text, store a file in the cloud, or identify the song playing in the background? There is, almost certainly, an API for that.

This shift towards a service-oriented architecture is one of the most significant productivity multipliers in modern development. By leveraging third-party APIs, we can deliver incredibly rich and complex functionality to our users without having to bear the enormous cost and complexity of building, maintaining, and scaling these specialized systems ourselves. We can stand on the shoulders of giants, integrating world-class payment processing from Stripe, robust cloud storage from Amazon Web Services, or powerful communication tools from Twilio directly into our applications. This chapter is about becoming a good citizen of that digital city. We will explore the tools and techniques for communicating with external services, from making the initial HTTP request to handling authentication, managing errors, and securely processing the data that flows back into our system.

At its most fundamental level, interacting with a web API is about making HTTP requests. Our PHP application acts as a client, sending a carefully crafted HTTP request to a URL provided by the third-party service and then parsing the response that comes back. While PHP has a built-in cURL extension that can handle this task, using it directly is often a verbose and cumbersome process, requiring you to manually set a dizzying array of options for headers, request bodies, and SSL verification. This approach is the equivalent of assembling a car from a pile of raw parts for every trip you want to take. The professional, modern approach is to use a dedicated HTTP client library that provides a clean, powerful, and object-oriented abstraction over the complexities of the HTTP protocol.

The undisputed standard for this in the PHP world is Guzzle. Guzzle is a comprehensive HTTP client that makes it trivial to send requests and work with their responses. More importantly, Guzzle is built on the standards established by the PHP-FIG. It uses PSR-7 objects to represent requests and responses and implements the PSR-18 `ClientInterface`. This means that if you write your code to depend on the standard PSR-18 interface rather than the concrete Guzzle class, you could swap out Guzzle for any other PSR-18 compliant client in the future with zero changes to your application logic. This adherence to community standards is a hallmark of a well-designed, decoupled system.

Let's begin by installing Guzzle and making a simple request to a public API, like the JSONPlaceholder API, which provides fake data for testing and prototyping.

```
composer require guzzlehttp/guzzle
```

Once installed, we can use a Guzzle client to perform a GET request to fetch a list of posts. A good practice is to manage the Guzzle client instance through our DI container, allowing it to be injected wherever it's needed.

```php
<?php

// Inside a controller or service class

use GuzzleHttp\Client;

use GuzzleHttp\Exception\GuzzleException;
```

```php
class PostService

{

    private Client $httpClient;


    public function __construct()

    {

        // In a real app, the Client would be injected.

        $this->httpClient = new Client(['base_uri' => 'https://jsonplaceholder.typicode.com']);

    }


    public function fetchAllPosts(): ?array

    {

        try {

            $response = $this->httpClient->get('/posts');


            if ($response->getStatusCode() === 200) {

                $body = $response->getBody()->getContents();
```

```php
        return json_decode($body,
true);
    }


        return null;


    } catch (GuzzleException $e) {

        // Handle connection errors,
timeouts, etc.

        // Log the error.

        return null;

    }

  }

}
```

This simple example demonstrates the core workflow. We instantiate a client, optionally with a base_uri to simplify our request URLs. We then call a method corresponding to the HTTP verb we want to use (like get, post, put, etc.). The get() method returns a PSR-7 Response object. We can then inspect this object's status code and, if it's successful, get the response body as a string, which we then decode from its JSON format into a PHP array. The entire operation is wrapped in a try...catch block to handle potential network failures gracefully.

Of course, most APIs are not public. They require you to prove your identity before they will share their data. The simplest form of this is using an **API Key**. An API key is a long, unique string that the service provides to you. Your application must include this key with every request it makes, and the service uses it to identify and authorize your application. The specific method for sending the key varies by service, but it is typically sent in one of two ways: as a custom HTTP header (e.g., `X-API-Key: YOUR_SECRET_KEY`) or as a query string parameter in the URL (e.g., `?apiKey=YOUR_SECRET_KEY`). Guzzle makes it easy to add headers or query parameters to all requests made by a client instance, which is perfect for this purpose.

A far more powerful and secure, but also more complex, authentication standard is **OAuth 2.0**. OAuth 2.0 is an authorization framework, not a simple authentication protocol. It's designed to allow a user of your application (the "resource owner") to grant your application (the "client") limited permission to access their data on a third-party service (the "resource server") without ever giving your application their password for that service. You see this every day when you click "Log in with Google" or "Sign in with Facebook."

The most common OAuth 2.0 flow for web applications is the "Authorization Code" flow. While the full specification is complex, the user's journey is relatively simple. First, the user clicks a "Connect to Service" button in your application. You redirect them to the third-party service's website, along with your application's client ID. The service asks the user to log in (if they aren't already) and then presents them with a consent screen, asking if they are willing to grant your application the requested permissions (e.g., "This app would like to read your profile information and access your photos"). If the user agrees, the service redirects them back to a "callback URL" that you previously configured, appending a temporary, single-use authorization code to the URL. Your application's server receives this request, extracts the code, and then makes a secure, direct, server-to-server request back to the service, exchanging the authorization code for a long-lived **access token**. It is this access token that you store and use to make authenticated API calls on the user's behalf, typically by sending it in the `Authorization: Bearer YOUR_ACCESS_TOKEN` header.

Implementing this multi-step dance from scratch is a complex and error-prone task. Fortunately, there is no need to. The PHP League provides an excellent, widely-used `oauth2-client` library that abstracts away the complexities of the protocol. You can pull in this generic client and then add a specific "provider" package for the service you want to integrate with (e.g., `league/oauth2-google`), which knows all the correct URLs and settings for that particular service. This library handles the redirects, the token exchange, and even the process of refreshing the access token when it expires, allowing you to focus on the business logic of your application.

As you begin to integrate with a service, it's a common anti-pattern to scatter API calls throughout your controllers and services. A much cleaner, more maintainable, and testable approach is to create a dedicated client class, sometimes called an SDK (Software Development Kit), for each third-party service you interact with. This class acts as a dedicated translator and gatekeeper, encapsulating all the specific knowledge required to talk to that one particular API.

This client class would receive its dependencies, such as a Guzzle client and the necessary API key, via its constructor. It would then expose a set of public methods that correspond to the business operations of the API, not the raw HTTP methods. For example, instead of having code elsewhere in your application that knows it needs to make a `POST` request to `/v1/charges` to process a payment, you would simply call `$stripeClient->createCharge($amount, $currency)`. This encapsulates the API's implementation details, like endpoint URLs and required parameters, in one place. If the API ever changes its endpoint from `/v1/charges` to `/v2/payments`, you only need to update it in one location: your `StripeClient` class.

This makes your application far more resilient to changes in the services it depends on.

One of the most critical aspects of interacting with external services is acknowledging that they are, by their very nature, unreliable. The network between your server and the API can fail. The API itself might be down for maintenance, overloaded, or might simply return an error. Your application must be built with this reality in mind; it must be resilient. Guzzle helps with this by throwing exceptions for HTTP responses with 4xx (client error) and 5xx (server error) status codes. Your code must always wrap its API calls in `try...catch` blocks to handle these exceptions gracefully. Catching a `GuzzleHttp\Exception\ClientException` allows you to inspect the response, parse any error message JSON provided by the API, and potentially provide a more helpful error message to your user.

Beyond simple error handling, you should also configure timeouts. A call to an external API should not be allowed to hang indefinitely, tying up one of your PHP processes. Guzzle allows you to set a `connect_timeout` (how long to wait to establish a connection) and a `timeout` (the total time allowed for the entire request). Setting sensible timeouts (e.g., a few seconds) is essential for preventing a slow third-party service from bringing your entire application to a grinding halt. For more advanced resilience, you can implement a **retry strategy**. If an API call fails with a transient error, like a temporary network blip or a `503 Service Unavailable` response, it often makes sense to automatically retry the request a second or third time before giving up. A common strategy is to use "exponential backoff," where you wait for a progressively longer period between each retry (e.g., 1 second, then 2 seconds, then 4 seconds). This can be implemented elegantly using Guzzle's middleware system, which allows you to wrap your requests with custom logic.

The conversation with a third-party service is not always one-way. For many types of events, it is inefficient for us to constantly poll an API asking, "Has anything happened yet?". This is where

webhooks come in. A webhook is a "reverse API." It is a mechanism that allows a third-party service to send your application an HTTP POST request when a specific event occurs on their end. For example, a payment gateway like Stripe can be configured to send a webhook to a URL on your server every time a charge succeeds, a subscription is canceled, or a dispute is opened. This allows your application to react to events in real time without the need for constant polling.

To handle a webhook, you create a dedicated public endpoint in your application—a route and a controller action—that is designed to receive these incoming POST requests. This endpoint has two critical responsibilities. The first is **security**. A webhook endpoint is a publicly accessible URL, and you must verify that any request it receives actually came from the third-party service and not from a malicious actor impersonating them. Services that provide webhooks almost always solve this with **signature verification**. When sending the webhook, the service will include a special HTTP header (e.g., Stripe-Signature) which contains a cryptographic signature. This signature is typically an HMAC hash of the raw request body, created using a secret key that is shared between you and the service. The very first thing your webhook controller must do is recalculate this signature using the same secret and algorithm and compare it to the signature from the header. If they do not match, the request is fraudulent and must be rejected immediately.

The second responsibility of a webhook handler is to be fast and responsive. The third-party service expects a quick acknowledgment that you have received the event, typically a 200 OK response. Your handler should not perform any slow or complex business logic directly. Doing so risks a timeout, which could cause the service to assume the delivery failed and retry sending the webhook, leading to duplicate processing. The best practice is to have your controller validate the signature, place the raw payload of the webhook into a background job queue (a topic we will touch on later when discussing scaling), and then immediately return a 200 OK response. A separate, asynchronous worker process can then pick the job up from the queue and safely perform the necessary business logic, such as updating an order status in your database or sending a confirmation email to the user.

Finally, it's worth noting that for many of the most popular and well-established services, you may not need to build your own API client or even work with Guzzle directly. Services like Stripe, AWS, Twilio, and SendGrid provide and maintain official PHP SDKs. These SDKs are pre-built libraries that you can install with Composer, and they provide a native PHP interface to the service's API. They handle authentication, error handling, and provide well-designed objects and methods for every feature the API offers. Whenever an official SDK is available, it is almost always the best choice. It is written and maintained by the people who know the API best, it will be kept up-to-date with new features, and it saves you the significant development and maintenance effort of building your own client. The principles you've learned in this chapter, however, are invaluable. They empower you to understand how those SDKs work under the hood, to debug them when things go wrong, and, most importantly, to confidently and professionally integrate with the thousands of other services that form the rich, interconnected fabric of the modern web.

CHAPTER TWENTY: Building and Consuming GraphQL APIs

For the past several chapters, we have operated within the world of REST. It is a world of resources, URLs, and HTTP verbs, a well-understood and powerful architectural style that has become the lingua franca of the modern web. We know that to fetch a user, we GET /users/123. To fetch their tasks, we GET /users/123/tasks. While this approach is clear and predictable, it has inherent limitations that become more pronounced as our applications grow in complexity, especially when dealing with rich, interconnected data models and diverse client needs, such as those of mobile apps or complex JavaScript frontends. This is where a different approach, a new dialect for API communication, offers a compelling alternative: GraphQL.

GraphQL is not a replacement for REST, nor is it a library or a framework. It is a query language for your API. Where REST exposes a multitude of endpoints for different resources, a GraphQL API typically exposes a single, powerful endpoint. The revolutionary idea at the heart of GraphQL is that it shifts the power of data fetching from the server to the client. Instead of the server dictating the structure and size of the response, the client sends a "query"—a declarative description of the exact data it needs, including nested relationships—and the server responds with a JSON object that precisely mirrors the structure of that query. This simple concept elegantly solves two of the most common problems that plague large-scale REST APIs: over-fetching and under-fetching.

Over-fetching occurs when an endpoint returns more data than the client actually needs. Imagine a mobile app that needs to display a list of task titles. A REST endpoint at GET /tasks might return an array of task objects, each containing the ID, title, full description, creation date, and completion status. The mobile client, only needing the title, is forced to download a larger payload, wasting bandwidth and slowing down the user experience. Under-fetching is the opposite problem. It's the "N+1 query" problem of the API world. To render a dashboard showing a user's profile and the titles of their five most recent tasks, a REST client would first have to hit `GET /users/me` to get the user data, and then, after that request completes, make a second request to `GET /users/123/tasks?limit=5`. This requires multiple network round trips, which is a significant performance killer, especially on mobile networks.

GraphQL solves both problems in a single, elegant stroke. The client can specify that it only wants the `title` from the list of tasks, eliminating over-fetching. It can also, in the same single query, ask for the current user's `name` and, nested within that, the `title` of their tasks, all at once. The server processes this query and returns all the requested information in one response, eliminating under-fetching and the need for multiple round trips. This client-driven approach makes GraphQL an incredibly efficient and flexible tool for building APIs that need to serve a diverse range of clients and evolve gracefully over time.

At the very heart of any GraphQL API is the schema. The schema is the central contract, the unambiguous source of truth that defines every capability of the API. It is written in a simple, human-readable format called the Schema Definition Language (SDL). The schema does not describe *how* to get the data, but rather *what* data is available. It defines the set of "types" that exist in your system and the relationships between them. This strong typing is a core feature of GraphQL, providing a level of introspection and self-documentation that is a massive boon for developers.

The schema is built from a few core concepts. The most fundamental are the object **Types**. A type defines a set of fields. For our application, we might define `User` and `Task` types. Each field within a type also has a type, which can be one of the built-in scalar types (`String`, `Int`, `Float`, `Boolean`, or `ID`) or another object type, which is how we create relationships. The exclamation mark (!) is used to denote that a field is non-nullable, meaning the server guarantees it will never return `null` for that field.

A basic schema for our application in SDL

```
type User {

id: ID!

name: String!

email: String!

tasks: [Task!]!

}

type Task {

id: ID!

title: String!

completed: Boolean!

user: User!

}
```

The schema also defines the entry points into the graph of data. For fetching data, these entry points are defined within a special type called `Query`. Each field on the `Query` type represents a top-level query that a client can make. For creating, updating, or deleting data, the entry points are defined within a `Mutation` type. This separation of read and write operations is a core convention in GraphQL.

```
type Query {
```

```
# Fetch a single task by its ID

task(id: ID!): Task

# Fetch a list of all tasks for the
authenticated user

tasks: [Task!]!

}

type Mutation {

# Create a new task

createTask(title: String!): Task!

}
```

This schema is the complete contract. Armed with this definition, a frontend developer can build their entire application, confident in the knowledge of what data they can ask for and what they will receive. Powerful tools like GraphQL Playground can introspect this schema and provide a full-featured, in-browser IDE for your API, complete with autocompletion and automatically generated documentation.

To bring this schema to life in PHP, we need a library that can parse GraphQL queries, validate them against our schema, and execute the necessary logic to fetch the data. The reference implementation and the foundation for most of the PHP GraphQL ecosystem is the `webonyx/graphql-php` library. This powerful library is responsible for the heavy lifting of the GraphQL specification, but it leaves one critical piece of the puzzle to us: telling it how to actually get the data. This is the job of the **resolver**.

A resolver is a PHP function that is responsible for providing the data for a single field in the schema. You can think of it as the glue between the abstract world of the GraphQL schema and the concrete world of your application's business logic—your repositories, services, and entity objects. When a query comes in, the graphql-php library walks the tree of requested fields, and for each field, it calls the corresponding resolver function. This resolver-per-field architecture is what makes GraphQL so flexible.

Let's build a simple GraphQL server using our existing Slim application. We'll start by installing the library: composer require webonyx/graphql-php. Our API will have a single endpoint, /graphql, which will be handled by a GraphQLController. This controller's job is to receive the incoming POST request (which contains the query), pass it to the GraphQL library for execution, and return the resulting JSON.

The core of the server-side setup is creating the schema object and providing a resolver map. The resolver map is an associative array where the keys correspond to types in our schema, and the values are another array of resolver functions for the fields of that type.

```php
<?php

// src/Controllers/GraphQLController.php


use GraphQL\GraphQL;

use GraphQL\Type\Schema;

use Psr\Http\Message\ResponseInterface as Response;

use Psr\Http\Message\ServerRequestInterface as Request;


class GraphQLController
```

```php
{
    // ... dependencies injected via
constructor (e.g., TaskRepository)


    public function handle(Request $request,
Response $response): Response

    {

        $schema = new Schema([

            'query' => /* Query Type
Definition */,

            'mutation' => /* Mutation Type
Definition */,

        ]);


        $input = $request->getParsedBody();

        $query = $input['query'];

        $variables = $input['variables'] ??
null;


        $rootValue = [

            'query' => [

                'tasks' => function ($root,
$args) {
```

```php
            // This is the resolver
for the 'tasks' query.

            // It calls our existing
business logic.

            return $this-
>taskRepository->findAllForCurrentUser();

        },

        'task' => function ($root,
$args) {

            return $this-
>taskRepository->findById($args['id']);

        }

    ],

    // ... mutation resolvers would
go here ...

    ];



    $result =
GraphQL::executeQuery($schema, $query,
$rootValue, null, $variables);

    $output = $result->toArray();



    $response->getBody()-
>write(json_encode($output));
```

```php
        return $response-
>withHeader('Content-Type',
'application/json');

    }

}
```

While it's possible to define the schema programmatically as shown above, it's often cleaner to write it in SDL and load it from a .graphql file. The more interesting part is how relationships are resolved. In our schema, a Task has a user field, and a User has a tasks field. We don't need a special resolver for every single field. If a field name in the schema matches a public property or a getter method on the PHP object returned by the parent resolver, graphql-php will resolve it automatically. For more complex relationships, we can provide a specific resolver. For example, to resolve the user field on a Task, the resolver function would receive the parent Task object as its first argument.

```php
<?php

// Part of a more complete resolver map

'Task' => [

    'user' => function ($task, $args) {

        // The $task variable is the result
of the parent resolver (the task
object/array).

        // We can use its user_id to fetch
the associated user.
```

```
        return $this->userRepository-
>findById($task['user_id']);

    }

]
```

This resolver-per-field approach naturally leads to a potential performance pitfall: the N+1 problem. Imagine a client requests a list of 10 tasks, and for each task, they also request the user's name. A naive implementation would result in 11 database queries: one to get the 10 tasks, and then 10 more queries (one for each task) to fetch the associated user. This is incredibly inefficient. The GraphQL community has solved this with a powerful concept known as the **DataLoader pattern**. A data loader is a utility that collects all the IDs that need to be fetched during a single GraphQL execution, de-duplicates them, and then fetches them all in a single, batched request (e.g., `SELECT * FROM users WHERE id IN (1, 2, 5, 8)`). It then distributes the results back to the individual resolvers that were waiting for them. This pattern is essential for building high-performance GraphQL APIs and is fully supported by the `webonyx/graphql-php` library.

Handling mutations is a very similar process. You define the mutation fields in your schema, often using dedicated `input` types to pass complex data structures as arguments. The resolver function for a mutation receives these arguments, performs the business logic (e.g., creates a new record in the database), and then returns the newly created or modified object. A key benefit of GraphQL mutations is that the client can request any data it needs about the changed object in the same round trip. After creating a new task, the client can immediately ask for its `id`, `title`, and even the `name` of its associated `user`, all in a single operation.

```
# An example mutation query
```

```
mutation CreateNewTask($title: String!) {

  createTask(title: $title) {

    id

    title

    completed

    user {

      id

      name

    }

  }

}
```

While building GraphQL servers is a common use case, it's also increasingly common for a PHP application to act as a client, consuming a GraphQL API provided by another service (either an internal microservice or a public API like GitHub's). The mechanics are fundamentally the same as interacting with any other web API. A GraphQL operation is simply an HTTP POST request to a single endpoint. The body of the request is a JSON object containing a query key (with the GraphQL query as a string) and, optionally, a variables key.

Using Guzzle, our HTTP client from the previous chapter, we can easily consume a GraphQL endpoint. A best practice when sending queries is to use variables. Instead of embedding user input directly into the query string, you use a placeholder in the query (e.g., $taskId) and send a separate JSON object containing the values for those variables. This prevents injection-style vulnerabilities and allows the GraphQL server to cache the parsed query structure.

```php
<?php

// Using Guzzle to consume a GraphQL API

use GuzzleHttp\Client;


$client = new Client();
$endpoint =
'https://api.example.com/graphql';


$query = <<<'GQL'

query GetTaskById($taskId: ID!) {

  task(id: $taskId) {

    id

    title

  }

}

GQL;


$response = $client->post($endpoint, [
```

```php
    'json' => [

        'query' => $query,

        'variables' => [

            'taskId' => '123'

        ]

    ]

]);
```

```php
$data = json_decode($response->getBody()-
>getContents(), true);

// $data will be ['data' => ['task' => ['id'
=> '123', 'title' => '...']]]
```

Finally, no discussion of GraphQL development would be complete without mentioning its extraordinary tooling. Because a GraphQL API is defined by a strongly-typed schema, it is possible to build powerful development tools that deeply understand the API's capabilities. The most important of these is **GraphiQL** (pronounced "graphical") and its modern successor, **GraphQL Playground**. These are in-browser IDEs that you can easily serve from your API's endpoint in a development environment. When you open one in your browser, it automatically introspects your schema and provides a multi-pane interface where you can write queries with full autocompletion, see the response in real time, and browse a complete, automatically generated documentation of every type, query, and mutation available. This tool alone dramatically speeds up the development and testing cycle for both backend and frontend developers, making the process of exploring and interacting with the API an interactive, discoverable experience.

GraphQL represents a powerful and flexible way to think about API design. It is not a universal solution, and the simplicity of REST is still the better choice for many resource-oriented APIs. But for applications with complex data relationships, a need to support a variety of client frontends, and a desire to minimize network traffic, GraphQL provides a robust, efficient, and increasingly popular set of tools and conventions. By understanding its core principles of schemas, queries, and resolvers, you can build APIs that are a joy for other developers to consume and that can evolve to meet the needs of your users for years to come.

CHAPTER TWENTY-ONE: Frontend Asset Bundling and Management

For the better part of this book, our focus has been squarely on the server. We have meticulously crafted a backend application that is secure, efficient, and well-architected. When we turned our attention to the user-facing part of the equation in Chapter Eleven, we used a powerful server-side templating engine, Twig, to render HTML. This is a classic and highly effective model. However, the expectations for a modern user interface have evolved dramatically. The frontend is no longer just a passive document that displays data; it is often a complex, interactive application in its own right, powered by a rich ecosystem of JavaScript and CSS.

As soon to be a modern PHP developer, you will be expected to work with a modern frontend. A simple web page might get away with a single `<link>` tag for a CSS file and a single `<script>` tag for some light interactivity. But a real application will have dozens, if not hundreds, of JavaScript modules, CSS components, images, and fonts. It will likely use a CSS pre-processor like Sass to write more maintainable styles and modern JavaScript syntax that isn't yet supported by all browsers. Simply linking all these files individually in your `base.html.twig` would be a performance disaster, forcing the user's browser to make a cascade of separate HTTP requests. It would also be a development nightmare to manage. To bridge this gap between a complex development environment and a lean, optimized production output, we need a frontend build process. We need tools to compile, optimize, and bundle our frontend assets into a handful of highly efficient files to be served to the user. This is the world of asset management.

It might seem strange that a book about PHP is about to take a deep dive into the world of JavaScript tooling, but this is the reality of the modern web stack. The entire ecosystem of modern frontend development tools—the compilers, the bundlers, the optimizers—is built on top of Node.js. Node.js is a JavaScript runtime that allows you to execute JavaScript on the server, and it comes with its own package manager, npm (Node Package Manager), which is the Composer of the frontend world. It is through npm that we will install and manage the tools needed to build our assets. For a professional PHP developer today, a working knowledge of the Node.js ecosystem is not optional; it is a required secondary skill set for delivering a complete application.

The core of our frontend workflow will be a tool called a bundler. For many years, the undisputed champion of this space was Webpack, an incredibly powerful and highly configurable tool that could be bent to any possible need. Its power, however, came at the cost of significant complexity. In recent years, a new tool has emerged that offers the same power for most common use cases but with a dramatically improved developer experience and staggering speed: Vite (pronounced "veet," the French word for "fast"). Vite has revolutionized the frontend development workflow by rethinking how assets are handled during development. It provides a near-instantaneous feedback loop that makes building user interfaces faster and more enjoyable. For this chapter, we will focus on Vite as our build tool of choice, as it represents the modern, state-of-the-art approach.

Let's begin by setting up a dedicated space for our frontend code. Inside our project's root directory, we'll create a new directory, which we can call `assets`. This will be the home for all our raw, uncompiled JavaScript, stylesheets, images, and fonts. The first step in any Node.js project is to create a `package.json` file. This file serves the exact same purpose as `composer.json`: it defines our project's metadata and, most importantly, lists our frontend dependencies. We can create it interactively with `npm init`, but for a simple setup, `npm init -y` will generate a default file for us.

Now, we can install Vite. It is a development dependency—a tool we need for building our application, but not one that needs to be on our production server—so we install it with the `--save-dev` flag.

```
npm install vite --save-dev
```

We'll also want to use a CSS pre-processor like Sass for its powerful features like variables and nesting. We can add it as another development dependency.

```
npm install sass --save-dev
```

Vite is configured using a simple JavaScript file at our project's root named `vite.config.js`. This is where we will tell Vite how to interact with our PHP application. For now, we will create a basic directory structure inside `assets`: one for JavaScript (`js`) and one for our Sass files (`scss`). We'll create our main entry points: `assets/js/app.js` and `assets/scss/app.scss`. These two files are the starting points for our entire frontend application. Every other JavaScript module or Sass partial we create will be imported, directly or indirectly, into these two files.

The true magic of Vite is its development server. When you are working on your application, you do not want to have to manually re-run a build command every single time you save a change to a CSS or JavaScript file. Instead, you run the Vite development server with a single command, which we'll add as a script to our `package.json`.

```
// package.json

{

  ...

  "scripts": {

    "dev": "vite",

    "build": "vite build"
```

```
    },

    . . .

}
```

Now, in your terminal, you can run `npm run dev`. This
command starts a lightweight, high-performance web server,
typically on a port like `localhost:5173`. This server's job is to
watch all of your asset files for changes. The revolutionary part is
what it does when a request comes in. Instead of bundling all your
JavaScript into a single file, the Vite dev server leverages native
ES Modules, a feature now built into all modern browsers. It
serves your JavaScript files individually, as they are requested by
the browser's `import` statements. This means there is no slow
bundling step. When you change a file, Vite only needs to process
that one file, not the entire application. This leads to near-
instantaneous updates in the browser, a feature known as Hot
Module Replacement (HMR). You can change a CSS color, and
without the page reloading, the new color will appear on screen.
This incredibly fast feedback loop is a massive boost to developer
productivity.

This, however, introduces a critical question: our PHP application
is running on its own server (perhaps `localhost:8080`), while
our assets are being served by the Vite dev server on
`localhost:5173`. How does our Twig template, rendered by
PHP, know how to load the assets from this separate server? The
answer requires a bit of wiring. During development, we need our
Twig layout file to output a special `<script>` tag that points to
the Vite client, which in turn knows how to load our `app.js`
entry point from the dev server.

```
<!-- In base.html.twig -->
```

```
<!-- Logic to check if we are in a
development environment -->

{% if getenv('APP_ENV') == 'development' %}

    <!-- 1. Point to the Vite client -->

    <script type="module"
src="http://localhost:5173/@vite/client"></s
cript>

    <!-- 2. Point to our main JS entry point
-->

    <script type="module"
src="http://localhost:5173/assets/js/app.js"
></script>

{% else %}

    <!-- Production asset tags will go here
-->

{% endif %}
```

With this in place, when you load your PHP application in the browser, the page will connect to the running Vite dev server and load your assets. You now have a seamless development experience where you can edit your Sass and JavaScript files and see the changes reflected instantly in your application, all rendered within the context of your real PHP backend.

The development server is a wonderful tool, but it is not what we use for production. For a production deployment, we need our assets to be as small and as fast as possible. This is the job of the build process. By running the npm run build command, we instruct Vite to prepare our assets for the harsh realities of the

303

public internet. This command kicks off a series of powerful optimizations.

First, Vite will follow every `import` statement from our `assets/js/app.js` and `assets/scss/app.scss` entry points to build a complete dependency graph of our entire frontend application. It will then compile our Sass files into standard CSS. It will transpile any modern JavaScript syntax into a more widely compatible version that will run correctly on older browsers. It will then perform a process called **bundling**, combining all of our separate JavaScript modules into one or a small number of files. This dramatically reduces the number of HTTP requests the browser needs to make.

Next, it will **minify** these bundled files, a process that removes all unnecessary characters—whitespace, comments, newlines—and shortens variable names, making the final file size as small as possible. It will also perform **tree-shaking**, an intelligent process that analyzes our code to detect and remove any functions or modules from our third-party libraries that we imported but never actually used. Finally, and most importantly for production, it will generate the output files with a unique hash in their filenames, for example, `app.a8f5b2c1.js`. This is a technique called **cache busting**. By changing the filename every time the content of the file changes, we can safely instruct browsers to cache our assets for a very long time. When we deploy a new version, the filename will be different, forcing the browser to download the new version instead of using a stale copy from its cache.

The result of this build process is a new directory, typically named `dist`, which contains our final, production-ready static assets. It will also contain a crucial file named `manifest.json`. This file is the Rosetta Stone that connects our development world to our production world. Because the output filenames have a random hash, we cannot simply hardcode them in our Twig template. The `manifest.json` file is a simple JSON map that tells us the final filename for a given source file.

```
// Example manifest.json

{

  "assets/js/app.js": {

    "file": "assets/app.a8f5b2c1.js",

    "src": "assets/js/app.js",

    "isEntry": true,

    "css": [ "assets/app.b3c2d1a0.css" ]

  },

  "assets/scss/app.scss": {

    "file": "assets/app.b3c2d1a0.css",

    "src": "assets/scss/app.scss"

  }

}
```

Our final task is to teach our PHP application how to read this manifest file in a production environment and generate the correct <script> and <link> tags. We can do this by creating a simple helper class or a custom Twig extension. This helper's job is to locate the manifest.json file, parse it, and provide a method that, given an entry point name like assets/js/app.js, returns the path to the final hashed file.

```
<?php
```

```php
// A simple helper class for the Vite
manifest

class ViteManifest

{

    private static array $manifest;


    public static function asset(string
$entry): string

    {

        if (!isset(self::$manifest)) {

            $manifestPath = __DIR__ .
'/../public/dist/manifest.json';

            self::$manifest =
json_decode(file_get_contents($manifestPath)
, true);

        }


        return '/dist/' .
self::$manifest[$entry]['file'];

    }


    // A similar method would be needed for
CSS files associated with an entry.
```

```
}
```

With this helper in place, we can complete the logic in our base.html.twig template. The final result is a system that intelligently switches between the two environments. In development, it loads assets from the fast Vite dev server. In production, it uses the manifest to load the fully optimized and cache-busted assets.

```
<!-- In base.html.twig -->

{% if getenv('APP_ENV') == 'development' %}

    <script type="module"
src="http://localhost:5173/@vite/client"></s
cript>

    <script type="module"
src="http://localhost:5173/assets/js/app.js"
></script>

{% else %}

    <!-- In a real app, this logic would be
in a cleaner Twig function -->

    <link rel="stylesheet" href="{{
vite_asset_css('assets/js/app.js') }}">

    <script type="module" src="{{
vite_asset_js('assets/js/app.js')
}}"></script>

{% endif %}
```

This dual-mode approach provides the best of both worlds. The development process is fluid and instantaneous, powered by HMR. The production output is lean, fast, and aggressively cacheable, delivering the best possible performance to your users. This workflow isn't limited to just JavaScript and CSS. When you reference an image or a font from within your CSS or JavaScript files (e.g., using `url('./images/logo.png')`), Vite's build process will automatically detect it. It will copy the image to the `dist` directory, potentially running optimizations on it, give it a hashed filename, and automatically rewrite the URL in your final CSS file to point to the correct location. This creates a completely self-contained build process where every asset your frontend needs is managed, optimized, and correctly referenced.

For larger applications, Vite also supports advanced techniques like **code splitting**. Instead of bundling all of your application's JavaScript into a single, monolithic file, Vite can be configured to split it into smaller, logical chunks. It can then generate code that will only load these chunks on demand. For example, the JavaScript needed for a complex admin dashboard might not be loaded until the user actually navigates to that section of the application. This significantly improves the initial page load time for the user, as they only have to download the code they need for the page they are currently viewing. The integration of a frontend build process is the final architectural piece in the puzzle of building a truly modern web application. It recognizes that the frontend and backend are two distinct but deeply connected parts of a single system. By establishing a clean, automated workflow for managing our frontend assets, we ensure that the user interface we deliver is as professional, performant, and maintainable as the PHP code that powers it from behind the scenes.

CHAPTER TWENTY-TWO: Continuous Integration and Continuous Deployment (CI/CD)

Our application is now a complex, multi-faceted system. It has a robust backend, a secure authentication layer, a well-defined frontend build process, and a containerized environment that ensures it runs consistently everywhere. We have a suite of automated tests that acts as our safety net, verifying the correctness of our code. The final piece of the puzzle is to bridge the gap between the code sitting on a developer's machine and that same code running flawlessly in production, serving real users. This last mile is often the most fraught with peril. Manual deployments are a recipe for human error—a forgotten step, a wrong command, a misconfigured server—all leading to downtime, stress, and a loss of user trust. To build and release software professionally, we must treat the deployment process not as a manual chore, but as an integral, automated, and reliable part of the application itself.

This is the domain of Continuous Integration and Continuous Deployment, a set of practices and philosophies that are universally abbreviated as CI/CD. It is the assembly line for modern software delivery. The core idea is to automate every step of the process that takes your code from a developer's commit to a live, running application. By doing so, we create a fast, reliable, and repeatable feedback loop. This automation doesn't just make deployments faster; it makes them safer. It codifies the process, ensuring that every single change, no matter how small, passes through the same rigorous gauntlet of quality checks and deployment steps every single time. It is the engine that allows development teams to move quickly and confidently, releasing new features and bug fixes not in large, risky batches, but as a continuous, predictable flow of value to the user.

At the heart of this philosophy are two distinct but deeply connected practices. **Continuous Integration (CI)** is the practice of frequently—often multiple times a day—merging all developers' working copies of code to a shared mainline repository. The "integration" part is key. Every time a developer pushes a new commit, an automated process is triggered. This process, known as a CI pipeline, is responsible for building the application and, most importantly, running the entire suite of automated tests against it. The primary goal of CI is to catch integration bugs early. If one developer's change breaks another developer's feature, the team knows about it in minutes, not in days or weeks. A successful CI run produces a "build artifact"—a packaged, tested, and verified version of the software that is ready to be deployed.

Continuous Deployment (CD) is the logical extension of CI. It takes the build artifact produced by a successful CI run and automatically deploys it to a production environment. This is the holy grail of automation, where every change that passes the automated tests is released to users without any human intervention. A slightly more conservative approach is **Continuous Delivery**, where the artifact is automatically deployed to a staging or pre-production environment, but a final, manual approval (often a single button click) is required to push it to the live production servers. Whether you choose delivery or deployment, the principle is the same: the process of releasing software should be a routine, low-stress, automated event, not a nerve-wracking, all-hands-on-deck ceremony. Our tests from Chapter Fifteen are the gatekeepers of this entire process, and our Docker image from Chapter Eighteen is the perfect, portable artifact to pass from one stage to the next.

The engine that drives this entire process is a CI/CD server. This is a tool that monitors your code repository for changes and executes the predefined steps of your pipeline. While there are many excellent options available, from the venerable and highly configurable Jenkins to the tightly integrated GitLab CI/CD, we will focus on one of the most popular and accessible choices for modern projects: GitHub Actions. As the built-in CI/CD platform for GitHub, it allows you to define your entire build, test, and deployment workflow in a simple YAML file that lives right alongside your application's code in the same repository.

The core concepts of GitHub Actions are straightforward. A **workflow** is the highest-level entity; it's the automated process you want to run. A workflow is defined in a YAML file in the `.github/workflows/` directory of your project. You can define what **events** will trigger the workflow, such as a `push` to a specific branch or the creation of a `pull_request`. A workflow is made up of one or more **jobs**. A job is a set of steps that execute on the same **runner**. A runner is simply a server (provided by GitHub or one you host yourself) that will execute your job. By default, jobs run in parallel, but you can configure them to depend on each other. Finally, each job consists of a sequence of **steps**. A step can be a simple command-line script or a reusable, pre-packaged unit of work called an **action**. The vast GitHub Marketplace provides thousands of actions built by the community and by GitHub itself, allowing you to easily perform complex tasks like setting up a specific version of PHP, logging into a Docker registry, or sending a Slack notification.

Let's construct a practical CI pipeline for our application. Our goal is to create a workflow that triggers on every push to our `main` branch or on any pull request. This pipeline will be responsible for checking out the code, setting up the PHP and Node.js environments, installing all our dependencies, running our static analysis and test suites, and finally, building our production Docker image. This workflow represents the "Continuous Integration" part of our strategy.

The first part of our YAML file, which we'll name `ci.yml`, defines the trigger conditions and the first job, which we'll call `test`. We'll specify that it should run on the latest version of Ubuntu.

```
name: CI Pipeline

on:
```

```yaml
push:

branches: [ "main" ]

pull_request:

branches: [ "main" ]

jobs:

test:

runs-on: ubuntu-latest
```

Now we define the steps for this job. The first step is always to check out the repository's code, which is done using the official `actions/checkout` action. Next, we need to set up our PHP environment. A fantastic community action, `shivammathur/setup-php`, makes this a one-liner. We'll also want to cache our Composer dependencies. Caching is a crucial optimization for CI pipelines. Installing all your Composer packages from scratch on every run can be slow. By caching the `vendor` directory, subsequent runs will only need to download packages if your `composer.lock` file has changed, dramatically speeding up the process.

```yaml
steps:

  - name: Checkout code

    uses: actions/checkout@v4


  - name: Setup PHP

    uses: shivammathur/setup-php@v2

    with:
```

```
        php-version: '8.3'

        extensions: pdo_mysql, zip # Add
extensions needed for your app

        tools: composer


    - name: Cache Composer dependencies

      uses: actions/cache@v4

      with:

        path: ~/.composer/cache/files

        key: ${{ runner.os }}-composer-${{
hashFiles('**/composer.lock') }}


    - name: Install Composer dependencies

      run: composer install --prefer-dist --
no-progress
```

With our backend dependencies installed, the next steps are to run our quality assurance checks. This is where our automated tests become the gatekeepers of our codebase. We'll add steps to run our static analysis tools and our PHPUnit test suite. If any of these steps fail (i.e., exit with a non-zero status code), GitHub Actions will immediately stop the workflow and report a failure. This provides the fast feedback that is central to CI. A pull request with a failing test suite can be blocked from merging, preventing bugs from ever reaching the main branch.

```
    - name: Run static analysis
```

```
run: ./vendor/bin/phpstan analyse src


- name: Run tests

  run: ./vendor/bin/phpunit
```

What about tests that need a database? Our integration tests from
Chapter Fifteen require a live database server to run. GitHub
Actions makes this remarkably easy to handle using a feature
called **service containers**. You can define a service that should be
started alongside your job's runner. For our purposes, we can tell
GitHub to start a MariaDB container. GitHub will handle creating
a network between the job runner and the service container,
allowing our tests to connect to the database using `localhost` as
the hostname. We simply need to pass the correct credentials as
environment variables to our test runner script.

```
jobs:

test:

runs-on: ubuntu-latest

services:

  mariadb:

    image: mariadb:10.6

    ports:

      - 3306:3306

    env:

      MYSQL_ROOT_PASSWORD: rootpassword
```

```yaml
        MYSQL_DATABASE: my_app_test

    options: --health-cmd="mysqladmin ping"
--health-interval=10s --health-timeout=5s --
health-retries=3



steps:

    # ... checkout and setup steps ...

    - name: Run tests

      run: ./vendor/bin/phpunit

      env:

        # These env vars will be available to
the phpunit process

        DB_HOST: 127.0.0.1

        DB_PORT: ${{
job.services.mariadb.ports }}

        DB_DATABASE: my_app_test

        DB_USERNAME: root

        DB_PASSWORD: rootpassword
```

After our backend tests pass, we need to handle our frontend assets. This involves setting up Node.js, caching our npm dependencies, and running our build script.

```yaml
    - name: Setup Node.js

      uses: actions/setup-node@v4
```

```
    with:

        node-version: '20'


    - name: Cache Node.js modules

      uses: actions/cache@v4

      with:

          path: ~/.npm

          key: ${{ runner.os }}-node-${{
hashFiles('**/package-lock.json') }}


    - name: Install npm dependencies

      run: npm install


    - name: Build frontend assets

      run: npm run build
```

The final step of a successful CI run is to produce the deployable artifact. For our containerized application, this artifact is a production-ready Docker image. We'll add steps to log in to a container registry (like Docker Hub or GitHub Container Registry) and then use the `docker/build-push-action` to build our production `Dockerfile` and push the resulting image to the registry, tagging it with a unique identifier like the Git commit SHA.

```yaml
- name: Log in to Docker Hub

  uses: docker/login-action@v3

  with:

    username: ${{
secrets.DOCKERHUB_USERNAME }}

    password: ${{ secrets.DOCKERHUB_TOKEN
}}


- name: Build and push Docker image

  uses: docker/build-push-action@v5

  with:

    context: .

    push: true

    tags: yourusername/my-app:${{
github.sha }}
```

Notice the use of `secrets`. You should never hardcode credentials in your workflow files. GitHub provides a secure vault for each repository where you can store sensitive information like API tokens and passwords. These are then made available to the workflow as encrypted variables.

With this workflow in place, we have achieved Continuous Integration. Every push to our repository now results in a fully tested, built, and packaged Docker image. The next logical step is to deploy it. This is where Continuous Deployment comes in. We can add a second job to our workflow that is responsible for deploying the application. We'll configure this job to run only after the `test` job has completed successfully, and only for pushes to the `main` branch, ensuring we never deploy broken code.

The simplest deployment strategy for a single-server application is to use SSH. The CD job will securely connect to our production server and execute a small script. This script will pull the new Docker image we just pushed to the registry, stop the currently running application container, and start a new container from the new image. A community action like `appleboy/ssh-action` makes this process straightforward.

```
deploy:

needs: test # This job will only run if the
'test' job succeeds

runs-on: ubuntu-latest

if: github.ref == 'refs/heads/main' # Only
run for pushes to the main branch



steps:

  - name: Deploy to production server

    uses: appleboy/ssh-action@master

    with:

      host: ${{ secrets.PROD_SERVER_HOST }}

      username: ${{
secrets.PROD_SERVER_USERNAME }}

      key: ${{ secrets.PROD_SERVER_SSH_KEY
}}
```

```
script: |

    cd /path/to/your/app

    docker pull yourusername/my-app:${{
github.sha }}

    docker stop my-app-container

    docker rm my-app-container

    docker run -d --name my-app-
container -p 80:80 yourusername/my-app:${{
github.sha }}
```

This simple `stop-and-start` deployment method does involve a few seconds of downtime while the container is being replaced. For many applications, this is perfectly acceptable. To achieve zero-downtime deployments, more advanced strategies like blue-green deployments are used, where the new version is started alongside the old one, and a load balancer is reconfigured to switch traffic over only after the new version is healthy. These strategies are often orchestrated by tools like Kubernetes, a topic we will touch upon when we discuss scaling.

By combining these workflows, we have created a complete, end-to-end pipeline that automates the entire lifecycle of a code change. A developer can push a single line of code, and minutes later, if it passes every quality gate, that change can be live in production, serving users. This automated process is the backbone of modern, high-velocity software development. It frees developers from the toil and risk of manual deployments, provides a rapid feedback loop that improves code quality, and ultimately enables a team to deliver better software, faster and more reliably than ever before. It is the invisible, tireless machinery that powers the modern web application.

CHAPTER TWENTY-THREE: Serverless PHP: A New Deployment Paradigm

For the entire history of web development, a fundamental truth has remained constant: to run a web application, you need a server. Whether it was a physical machine humming in a data center, a virtual machine rented from a cloud provider, or a Docker container orchestrated by Kubernetes, the core model involved provisioning, configuring, and maintaining a long-running environment that waited patiently for incoming requests. This paradigm is powerful and well-understood, but it carries an inherent operational cost. You are responsible for the server's health, its security, its operating system patches, and, critically, you pay for it to be running 24/7, even if it only receives a handful of requests per day. Serverless computing presents a radical and compelling alternative. It is a cloud-native deployment model that seeks to abstract away the server entirely, allowing you to run your code without ever thinking about the underlying infrastructure.

The term "serverless" is, of course, a notorious misnomer. There are, and always will be, servers involved. The revolutionary idea is that you no longer have to manage them. Serverless computing, most commonly realized through a model called Function-as-a-Service (FaaS), shifts the responsibility of all infrastructure management to the cloud provider. Instead of deploying a complete application to a running server, you deploy individual pieces of your application's logic as isolated "functions." The cloud provider takes care of everything else. When a request comes in that is meant for your function, the provider dynamically provisions a micro-container, executes your code within it, and then shuts it down. This simple, event-driven model introduces a groundbreaking new economic and operational reality. You pay not for idle server time, but only for the precise number of milliseconds your code is actually running. The scaling is, in theory, infinite and completely automatic. If your function receives one request or one million requests, the provider handles it, transparently spinning up as many instances as are needed to meet the demand.

For many years, the PHP community looked upon the rise of serverless with a degree of skepticism. The very nature of the serverless execution model seemed at odds with PHP's traditional identity. PHP was designed for a shared-nothing, request-response world where a script is born, lives for a few dozen milliseconds, and then dies, cleaning up all its resources. The serverless model, with its concept of "cold starts"—the initial delay required to spin up a new container for the first time—seemed to penalize languages like PHP that rely on bootstrapping a full framework on every request. Early serverless platforms were heavily optimized for languages like Node.js and Python, which were better suited to the event-driven, long-running process model.

However, two powerful forces have converged to make serverless PHP not just a possibility, but a practical and potent deployment strategy. The first is the staggering performance evolution of PHP itself. The speed and efficiency gains from PHP 7 and PHP 8 have dramatically reduced the "cold start" penalty, making framework bootstrapping significantly faster. The second, and more transformative, force has been the innovation within both the PHP community and the cloud platforms themselves. Projects have emerged that create a seamless bridge between the traditional PHP world and the serverless environment, while cloud providers have introduced new capabilities, like running functions from Docker container images, that give PHP developers a first-class seat at the serverless table.

The undisputed leader in the serverless space is Amazon Web Services (AWS) with its Lambda service. AWS Lambda is the archetypal FaaS platform. You upload your code as a Lambda function, and you configure an "event source" to trigger it. While this event source can be almost anything in the AWS ecosystem— a new file uploaded to an S3 bucket, a message on a queue, a scheduled cron job—the most common trigger for a web application is an HTTP request. This is handled by another service, Amazon API Gateway, which acts as the public-facing front door, receiving HTTP requests and translating them into an "event" payload that it passes to your Lambda function for execution. The function processes this event, returns a response payload, and API Gateway translates that back into an HTTP response for the user.

A PHP Lambda function is, at its core, a script with a single entry point known as a handler. The Lambda runtime environment executes this script and passes it an event object (containing all the details of the incoming request) and a context object (with information about the invocation). Your handler's job is to process this event and return an array that conforms to the structure API Gateway expects for a response. While it's possible to build a custom runtime to handle this interaction from scratch, the modern PHP community has overwhelmingly coalesced around a brilliant open-source project that makes this entire process feel almost magical: Bref.

Bref (which means "brief" in French) is a Composer package and an accompanying set of open-source tools that are designed to make deploying serverless PHP applications on AWS Lambda as simple and seamless as possible. It provides pre-built, highly optimized PHP runtimes as Lambda layers, effectively solving the problem of how to get PHP running in the first place. More importantly, it provides a clean, elegant integration that allows you to take an existing PHP web application, built with a framework like Slim or Laravel, and run it on Lambda with minimal, and sometimes zero, changes to your application's code. Bref acts as the adapter, the universal translator that sits between the AWS Lambda execution model and the PSR-7/PSR-15 standards that our modern PHP applications already speak.

To deploy an application with Bref, you typically use the Serverless Framework, a popular open-source command-line tool for building and deploying serverless applications across different cloud providers. You define your entire serverless infrastructure—your functions, their triggers, and their permissions—in a single YAML file named `serverless.yml`. This file becomes the codified, version-controlled definition of your application's deployment.

A `serverless.yml` for our Slim API, configured to use Bref, would be surprisingly simple. We would specify AWS as the provider, add the Bref plugin, and then define our function. Instead of creating a separate function for every single route, Bref allows for a more monolithic approach that is a natural fit for PHP frameworks. We define a single Lambda function that will run our entire application. We configure its "handler" to be a specific file that Bref provides, and we set its event trigger to catch all HTTP requests (`httpApi: '*'`).

```yaml
# serverless.yml

service: my-modern-php-app


provider:

    name: aws

    region: us-east-1

    runtime: provided.al2 # Use Bref's
provided Amazon Linux 2 runtime


plugins:

    - ./vendor/bref/bref


functions:

    api:
```

```
handler: public/index.php

description: 'Our entire Slim API
running on a single Lambda function'

layers:

    # Use one of Bref's pre-built
PHP 8.3 FPM layers

    - ${bref:layer.php-83-fpm}

events:

    - httpApi: '*' # Catch all HTTP
requests
```

The magic is in the `handler: public/index.php` line.
Bref's FPM layer intelligently spins up a lightweight version of the
PHP-FPM process inside the Lambda container. When API
Gateway sends a request, Bref's runtime receives it, translates it
into a standard FastCGI request, and passes it to your
`index.php` file, the very same front controller we have been
using all along. Your Slim application boots up, receives a
standard PSR-7 `Request` object, processes it through your
middleware and controllers, and returns a PSR-7 `Response`
object, completely oblivious to the fact that it is running inside a
transient, serverless environment. Bref handles the final step of
translating that response back into the format Lambda expects.
With this configuration in place, deploying your entire application
to a globally scalable, pay-per-use infrastructure is a single
command: `serverless deploy`.

This elegant abstraction, however, rests on a fundamental
architectural constraint that you must respect: **serverless functions
must be stateless**. The ephemeral nature of the FaaS execution
model means you cannot assume that anything you write to the
local filesystem will be there for the next request. You cannot rely

on in-memory state, as a subsequent request might be handled by a completely different container on a different physical machine. Any state that needs to persist between requests must be externalized. Your database, such as Amazon RDS, is an external state store. Your user sessions, if you need them, should be stored in a service like Redis or DynamoDB. File uploads must be sent directly to a dedicated object storage service like Amazon S3. This enforcement of statelessness is not a limitation; it is a best practice that leads to more scalable and resilient applications, regardless of the deployment model.

One of the most significant practical challenges of running a traditional PHP application in a serverless environment is managing database connections. A standard application might maintain a persistent pool of connections to the database. In a serverless world, where thousands of function instances could potentially spin up to handle a traffic spike, you could easily overwhelm your database with a flood of new connection requests. This is a problem that requires a specific solution, such as Amazon RDS Proxy. RDS Proxy is a managed service that sits between your Lambda functions and your database. It maintains a warm pool of connections to the database, and your functions connect to the proxy instead of directly to the database. This allows your application to scale to massive levels of concurrency without exhausting the database's connection limits, solving one of the key architectural hurdles for serverless PHP.

The serverless model also encourages a shift in thinking about your application's architecture. While running your entire framework as a single "Lambda-lith" is a perfectly valid and highly effective starting point, the FaaS model also excels at running small, single-purpose functions. This aligns perfectly with an event-driven or microservices architecture. For example, you could have a Lambda function whose sole purpose is to resize an image. Its trigger would be a file upload event from an S3 bucket. When a user uploads a large image, S3 automatically triggers your function. The function, which contains only the image manipulation logic, reads the new file, generates several thumbnail sizes, and saves them back to another S3 bucket. This entire process happens asynchronously, without ever blocking your main application, and you pay only for the few hundred milliseconds of compute time it takes to resize that one image.

So, when is serverless the right choice for your PHP application? It excels in scenarios with unpredictable or "spiky" traffic. An API for a mobile app that is busy in the morning and evening but quiet overnight is a perfect use case. Webhook handlers, which receive infrequent but important POST requests from third-party services, are another ideal fit. Scheduled tasks or cron jobs that need to run once an hour or once a day can be implemented as a Lambda function triggered by a scheduler, costing pennies to run instead of requiring a server to be active 24/7 just for that task. For applications with very steady, predictable, high-volume traffic, the cost model of a dedicated, provisioned server might still be more economical. Similarly, applications that require long-lived, persistent connections, like the WebSocket server we built in Chapter Fourteen, are not a natural fit for the short-lived FaaS model and are better suited to a container-based or traditional server deployment.

The rise of tools like Bref and the increasing sophistication of cloud platforms have transformed serverless from a curious novelty into a powerful and strategic tool in the modern PHP developer's arsenal. It offers an unparalleled combination of scalability, operational simplicity, and cost efficiency for a wide range of applications. It forces you to embrace best practices like statelessness and dependency injection, leading to cleaner, more maintainable code. By abstracting away the tedious and undifferentiated work of managing servers, it allows you to focus on what truly matters: writing the code that delivers unique value to your users. It is a paradigm that embodies the promise of the cloud, offering a glimpse into a future where infrastructure is truly invisible, and the only thing that matters is the application itself.

CHAPTER TWENTY-FOUR: Scaling Your PHP Application

We have built a modern, professional web application. It is well-tested, secure, containerized, and deployed through an automated pipeline. It works beautifully. But what happens when our application becomes a victim of its own success? What happens when the trickle of initial users turns into a steady stream, and then a flood? An architecture designed for a hundred users will buckle under the weight of a hundred thousand. The application will slow to a crawl, the database will become unresponsive, and users will be greeted with timeouts and error pages. This is the challenge of scalability: the process of designing and evolving a system to gracefully handle a significant and growing amount of load.

Scaling is not a single action but a continuous journey of identifying and eliminating bottlenecks. A bottleneck is any component in your system that constrains the overall throughput. At first, it might be the CPU on your single server. Once you fix that, it might become the database's ability to handle connections. Fix that, and it might be the time it takes to process a file upload. Scaling is an iterative process of finding the next weakest link in the chain and reinforcing it. In this chapter, we will explore the fundamental strategies and architectural patterns that allow a PHP application to grow from a single server to a distributed, resilient system capable of serving millions of users.

The Two Dimensions of Scaling: Up vs. Out

When an application starts to slow down under load, the first and most intuitive response is to make the server more powerful. This is known as **vertical scaling**, or "scaling up." It involves adding more resources—a faster CPU, more RAM, a speedier SSD—to the single machine that runs your application. In the world of cloud computing, this often means simply shutting down your virtual server and restarting it on a larger, more expensive instance type.

Vertical scaling is attractive because of its simplicity. For a while, it works wonderfully. Your code doesn't need to change, and your architecture remains the same. You are simply running the same application on a bigger box. This approach, however, has two fundamental limitations. The first is cost. The price of high-end server instances increases exponentially; doubling the power often more than doubles the cost. The second, and more critical, limitation is that you will eventually hit a physical ceiling. There is a finite amount of CPU and RAM you can pack into a single machine. More importantly, vertical scaling does nothing to address the issue of having a single point of failure. If that one, incredibly powerful server goes down for any reason, your entire application is offline.

This leads us to the second, more powerful dimension of scaling: **horizontal scaling**, or "scaling out." Instead of making one server bigger, we add more servers. We distribute the load across a fleet of multiple, often smaller and less expensive, machines. This approach is the cornerstone of virtually every large-scale web application on the internet today. It provides a path to almost limitless scalability; if you need more capacity, you simply add more servers to the pool. It also dramatically improves reliability. If one server in the fleet fails, the others can pick up the slack, and the application can continue to function without a catastrophic outage. Horizontal scaling is more complex to implement than its vertical counterpart, as it forces us to rethink our application's architecture, but it is the only viable path for building a truly scalable and resilient system.

Horizontal Scaling in Practice: The Load Balancer and the Stateless Application

The linchpin of any horizontally scaled architecture is the **load balancer**. A load balancer is a specialized piece of software or hardware that acts as the application's front door. All incoming traffic from users is directed to the load balancer's single, public IP address. The load balancer's job is to inspect this traffic and intelligently distribute it across the pool of identical application servers, which are often called "web nodes" or "app nodes." It constantly monitors the health of these nodes, directing traffic only to the healthy ones and taking any failed servers out of rotation until they recover. This simple mechanism is what allows a fleet of servers to act as a single, cohesive unit from the user's perspective.

For this model to work, there is one absolute, non-negotiable requirement: the application servers themselves must be **stateless**. This is a concept we encountered in the serverless world, and it is just as critical here. Statelessness means that any single application server can handle any user's request at any time, because no important, user-specific data is stored on the local server itself. If a user's first request is handled by Server A, and their second request five seconds later is handled by Server B, the experience should be seamless. This has several profound architectural implications.

The first challenge is managing user sessions. The default PHP session handler stores session data in files on the local disk of the server. This immediately breaks our stateless requirement. If Server A creates a session file for a user who has just logged in, Server B has no access to that file and will treat the user's next request as if they were an anonymous guest. The solution is to externalize session storage. Instead of storing session data locally, all application servers must be configured to store it in a centralized, shared data store that every server can access. A fast in-memory store like Redis or Memcached is the perfect tool for this job. By configuring `php.ini` to use a Redis session handler, the state of the user's session is no longer tied to a specific server, allowing the load balancer to distribute requests freely.

The second challenge is handling file uploads. Just like session files, if a user uploads a profile picture and it gets saved to the local disk of Server A, that image will be unavailable when a request to view it is later handled by Server B. The solution, again, is to use a centralized, shared storage system. While a network-attached storage solution like NFS can work, it can also become a performance bottleneck and a single point of failure itself. The modern, cloud-native solution is to use an object storage service. Services like Amazon S3 or DigitalOcean Spaces provide a highly scalable, durable, and cost-effective API for storing and retrieving files. When a user uploads a file, your PHP application should not save it locally. Instead, it should stream the file directly to the object storage service. The file is then served to users via a separate, globally distributed CDN, which takes a huge amount of load off your application servers.

With session handling and file storage externalized, our application servers become true, interchangeable cattle, not pets. We can add new ones to the pool or remove failed ones at will, and the application as a whole remains consistent and available. Our Docker containers from Chapter Eighteen are the perfect building blocks for these stateless nodes. We can use a single, tested Docker image as the blueprint to launch as many identical application server containers as we need to handle the current load.

The Next Bottleneck: Scaling the Database

By successfully scaling our application tier horizontally, we have solved one problem, but in doing so, we have created another. We have simply moved the bottleneck. With dozens or hundreds of application servers all capable of handling requests, the new single point of failure and the most likely performance constraint is our single database server. No matter how powerful we make it (vertical scaling), a single database can only handle a finite number of connections and queries. To scale the data layer, we must also apply the principles of horizontal scaling, but the stateful nature of a database makes this a more delicate operation.

The first and most common strategy for scaling a database is to separate read and write operations by using **read replicas**. Most web applications have a workload that is heavily skewed towards reads. A typical social media application might have thousands of users reading posts and comments for every one user who is writing a new post. We can take advantage of this asymmetry by creating one or more read-only copies of our main database, called replicas.

The architecture is known as a primary-replica (formerly master-slave) setup. You have one **primary** database that is the single source of truth. All INSERT, UPDATE, and DELETE queries— any operation that writes data—must be sent to this primary database. The primary database is then configured to asynchronously replicate all of its changes to one or more **replica** databases. Your application code is then modified to direct all of its SELECT queries—any operation that only reads data—to these replicas. This simple change can dramatically reduce the load on your primary database, freeing it up to focus on the more intensive work of processing writes.

Implementing this requires changes at the application level. Your database connection configuration needs to be aware of both the primary and the replica servers. A sophisticated data access layer or ORM can be configured to automatically route queries based on their type. For example, you might have one PDO connection object for writes and another that load balances read queries across a pool of replica connections. A critical consideration with this model is **replication lag**. The process of copying data from the primary to the replicas is incredibly fast, but it is not instantaneous. There might be a delay of a few milliseconds or even seconds. This means it's possible for your application to write a piece of data to the primary and then immediately try to read it from a replica before it has arrived, resulting in not-found errors or stale data. Your application must be designed to tolerate this eventual consistency, for example, by directing a user's reads to the primary database for a short period immediately after they have performed a write operation.

For the vast majority of applications, a primary-replica architecture provides more than enough database scalability for years. However, for applications that reach a truly massive scale, even the primary database's ability to handle writes can become a bottleneck. The solution to this is a far more complex technique called **database sharding**. Sharding involves horizontally partitioning your data across multiple, independent databases. Instead of one giant users table, you might have four users shards, where users with IDs 1-1,000,000 are on Shard 1, users

1,000,001-2,000,000 are on Shard 2, and so on. The application logic becomes responsible for knowing which shard to query to find a particular piece of data. While sharding offers almost limitless write scalability, it introduces immense operational complexity in areas like schema changes, cross-shard queries, and backups. It is a strategy to be considered only when all other avenues of database optimization and read scaling have been exhausted.

Decoupling with Asynchronous Work: The Job Queue

One of the most effective ways to improve the perceived performance and the actual scalability of your application is to not do slow work during a user's web request. A web request should be as fast and responsive as possible. Any task that is time-consuming and doesn't need to be completed immediately before showing the user a response is a prime candidate for being offloaded to a background process. This is the role of a **job queue**.

A job queue provides a mechanism for asynchronous communication between different parts of your system. The architecture consists of three main parts. Your web application acts as the **producer**. When a slow task needs to be performed, such as sending a welcome email after a user registers or processing a video that has just been uploaded, the application doesn't perform the task itself. Instead, it creates a "job"—a message that contains all the information needed to perform the task (e.g., the user's ID and the email template to use)—and pushes it onto a **queue**. The queue is a message broker, a service like Redis or RabbitMQ, that acts as an intermediary buffer. Finally, you have one or more **worker** processes. A worker is a separate, long-running PHP script, often started from the command line, whose only job is to listen to the queue. It acts as the **consumer**, pulling jobs off the queue one by one and executing the actual task.

This decoupling has profound benefits. First, it makes your web application feel dramatically faster to the user. The registration process, from the user's perspective, is now instantaneous. They get a "Success!" message immediately, while the slower work of sending the email happens a few seconds later in the background. Second, it improves reliability. If your email service's API is temporarily down, the worker can be configured to retry the job later without ever having caused an error during the user's initial web request. Third, it provides a new and powerful dimension for scaling. If you find that jobs are piling up in the queue faster than they can be processed, you don't need to scale your web servers; you simply need to start more worker processes to increase the processing throughput.

This architecture—a load balancer distributing traffic to a pool of stateless application nodes, which in turn communicate with a centralized cache, a primary-replica database cluster, an object store, and a job queue serviced by background workers—is the standard blueprint for a modern, scalable web application. It is a system of specialized, decoupled components, each of which can be scaled independently, allowing you to precisely target and eliminate bottlenecks as your application grows. It transforms your application from a fragile monolith into a resilient, distributed system capable of weathering the storms of internet-scale traffic.

CHAPTER TWENTY-FIVE: The Future of PHP: What's Next?

We have arrived at the final leg of our journey. Over the past twenty-four chapters, we have dismantled and reassembled the modern PHP application, piece by piece. We have moved from the foundational syntax of the language to the complex orchestration of containerized, scalable, and continuously deployed systems. The picture we have painted is of a language that is vibrant, mature, and profoundly capable in the landscape of 2025. But the landscape of technology is never static. It is a place of constant, relentless motion. The moment a language ceases to evolve is the moment it begins its slow march toward obsolescence. PHP has avoided this fate for three decades precisely because it has never stood still.

This final chapter is not a retrospective, but a forecast. Our goal is to look over the horizon and glimpse the direction in which the language and its ecosystem are moving. We will explore the concrete features being forged for the next version of PHP, the long-term architectural ideas being debated for future generations of the language, and the broader trends in tooling and architecture that will shape the life of a PHP developer in the years to come. The story of modern PHP is one of continuous improvement, and the next chapter of that story is already being written.

The Predictable Cadence: The Annual Release Cycle

Before looking at specific features, it is important to appreciate one of the most significant structural changes in PHP's modern era: the predictable, annual release cycle. Gone are the days of long, unpredictable gaps between major versions. Since the release of PHP 7.0, the community has adhered to a disciplined, clockwork-like schedule. A new minor version of the language is released in late November or early December of every year. Each version is actively supported with bug fixes for two years, followed by a third and final year of security fixes only. This predictable rhythm has been a monumental boon for the entire ecosystem.

It provides a clear roadmap for developers, businesses, and hosting providers. We know when to expect new features, and we have a clear timeline for managing upgrades and handling deprecations. This stability allows framework and library authors to plan their own release schedules in alignment with the language, ensuring that the tools we rely on can take advantage of new language features in a timely manner. This professionalization of the release process is a quiet but powerful testament to the maturity of the language. It is the stable foundation upon which all future evolution is built.

As we look toward the immediate future, the features destined for the next version, PHP 8.4, are already taking shape through the Request for Comments (RFC) process. This is the open, democratic forum where core developers and community members propose, debate, and vote on new features for the language. While the final feature set is always subject to the outcomes of these votes, the active RFCs give us a clear window into the community's priorities. One of the most anticipated features being discussed is the introduction of Property Hooks. This RFC proposes a mechanism to allow developers to run custom code whenever a class property is read from or written to, providing a clean, built-in way to implement patterns like mutation observers or computed properties without the boilerplate of explicit getter and setter methods.

Another area of focus is the continued refinement of the type system. Proposals are often floated to add more expressive power, such as typed class constants or more advanced generic-like features, building on the foundations of union and intersection types. The standard library is also a constant source of incremental improvement. New functions are regularly added to simplify common tasks, and existing functions are sometimes given new, more powerful signatures. These yearly updates are typically not revolutionary, but evolutionary. They are a series of deliberate, thoughtful refinements that sand down the rough edges of the language and provide developers with more powerful and expressive tools for their daily work.

The Long View: The Road to PHP 9

While minor versions bring refinement, major versions provide an opportunity for deeper, more structural changes. The journey from PHP 7 to PHP 8 brought us the JIT compiler and a host of powerful new syntax features. The eventual arrival of PHP 9, while still several years away, is the subject of ongoing discussion and will likely focus on cleaning up the language's historical baggage and paving the way for the next decade of development.

A major version is the only time the language can introduce backward-compatibility breaks. This is a power that the core team wields with extreme caution, but it is necessary for the long-term health of the language. One of the primary goals for a future major version will be to address long-standing inconsistencies in the standard library. This might involve renaming functions for consistency (for example, standardizing the order of the "needle" and "haystack" arguments in string and array functions), removing old, deprecated aliases, and reorganizing functions into more logical namespaces. These changes, while potentially causing some upgrade friction, are essential for making the language easier to learn and more predictable to use.

The type system is another area ripe for long-term evolution. While PHP's gradual, opt-in type system is one of its greatest strengths, there is a strong desire in the community to push it further. The long-term dream for many is the introduction of full, user-land generics, a feature that would allow developers to write code that is more flexible and type-safe when working with collections and data structures. This is an incredibly complex feature to implement in a dynamically-typed language, and it is a challenge the core team is approaching with deliberate care, learning from the implementations in other languages like TypeScript and C#.

A significant force guiding this long-term vision is The PHP Foundation. Established in late 2021 and supported by a coalition of major companies in the ecosystem, the foundation's mission is to ensure the long-term health and prosperity of the language by funding core developers. This has been a transformative development. It provides a stable financial backing for developers to work on the less glamorous but critically important tasks of maintenance, bug fixing, and long-term architectural planning. The foundation's existence ensures that the evolution of PHP is not left to the spare time of volunteers but is a sustained, professional engineering effort.

The Unrelenting Pursuit of Performance

The dramatic performance leap with the release of PHP 7 was a watershed moment that silenced many of the language's critics. This focus on performance has not waned. The introduction of the Just-In-Time (JIT) compiler in PHP 8 was a significant statement of intent. While its initial implementation provided the most benefit for long-running, CPU-intensive tasks rather than the typical short-lived web request, the work on the JIT is an ongoing project.

Future development of the JIT is likely to focus on making it more effective for the common web application workload. This is a complex challenge, as the short-lived nature of a web request makes it difficult for the JIT to "warm up" and gather enough information to make effective optimization decisions. Researchers and core developers are exploring different strategies, including the possibility of a "tracing" JIT that is better suited to this kind of workload, as well as finding ways to share JIT-compiled code between different PHP-FPM worker processes. While these are long-term research projects, they signal a clear commitment to ensuring PHP remains one of the fastest and most efficient dynamically-typed languages in the world.

This pursuit of performance is not limited to the core of the language. It is also the driving force behind the continued growth of the asynchronous PHP ecosystem. The introduction of Fibers in

PHP 8.1 provided a native, low-level mechanism for building lightweight concurrency, a feature that asynchronous frameworks like Amp and Swoole have enthusiastically adopted. This has made writing asynchronous, coroutine-based code more ergonomic and efficient than ever before.

As this paradigm matures, we are likely to see its adoption grow beyond the niche of high-concurrency network services. Libraries and framework components may begin to offer asynchronous, non-blocking alternatives for common I/O operations, such as making HTTP requests or interacting with a database. While the traditional synchronous model will likely remain the default for its simplicity, the increasing availability and ease of use of asynchronous tools will give developers a powerful option for squeezing the maximum possible performance out of their servers for I/O-bound tasks.

A Maturing Toolchain: The Rise of Static Analysis

Perhaps the most significant trend in the broader PHP ecosystem is the move towards a more disciplined, type-safe, and statically-analyzed style of development. While PHP remains a dynamically-typed language at its core, the optional type system has been so widely and enthusiastically embraced that it is now the de facto standard for any modern application. This cultural shift has been supercharged by the rise of incredibly powerful static analysis tools like Psalm and PHPStan.

These tools, as we have discussed, act as a layer of verification on top of the PHP language itself. They can understand advanced type information from docblocks, analyze the flow of your code to find potential bugs, and enforce a level of correctness that the PHP runtime alone does not. The future of these tools is one of deeper integration and more powerful inference. They are becoming more adept at understanding complex framework-specific magic, and their ability to define and check for generic-like types through annotations provides a powerful glimpse into the future of type-safe PHP.

We are likely to see these tools become an even more standard, non-negotiable part of the professional PHP developer's workflow, just as Composer and PHPUnit are today. Frameworks and libraries are increasingly shipping with their own static analysis configuration files, and CI pipelines are being configured to fail a build not just on a failing test, but on a "type error" detected by Psalm or PHPStan. This trend represents a maturation of the ecosystem, a move towards a development culture that values correctness, predictability, and the proactive prevention of bugs before the code is ever run.

PHP's Enduring Place in a Polyglot World

The web development landscape of today is a polyglot one. The idea of a single "best" language for every task has been replaced by a more nuanced understanding of using the right tool for the right job. High-performance, real-time services might be written in Go or Rust. Data science and machine learning tasks are the domain of Python. And the frontend is, and will remain, the kingdom of JavaScript. So, where does this leave PHP?

The future of PHP is one of embracing its strengths. It remains, arguably, the fastest and easiest way to build robust, data-driven web applications and APIs. The simplicity of its deployment model, the unparalleled richness of its package ecosystem via Composer, and the massive, global community of developers and open-source projects give it an enduring and powerful advantage. Frameworks like Laravel and Symfony continue to innovate at a staggering pace, providing elegant, productive, and powerful solutions to the common problems of web development.

PHP's future is not about trying to be the best language for everything. It is about being the best language for its core domain: the web. It is about providing a pragmatic, productive, and high-performance platform for building the vast majority of applications that businesses and users need every day. The language is evolving to be more robust, more performant, and more pleasant to write. The ecosystem is maturing, adopting best practices from across the software engineering world. The community is thriving, backed by the stability of The PHP Foundation. After three decades, the persistent rumors of PHP's demise continue to be, as they have always been, greatly exaggerated. The language is not just surviving; it is actively, enthusiastically, and powerfully building the future of the web.

---

www.ingramcontent.com/pod-product-compliance
Lightning Source LLC
LaVergne TN
LVHW022334060326
832902LV00022B/4028